FOR ORGANS, PIANOS & ELECTRONIC KEYBOARDS

E-Z PLAY TODAY 123

POP PIANO HITS

ISBN 978-1-4234-8101-0

HAL•LEONARD® CORPORATION

7777 W. BLUEMOUND RD. P.O. BOX 13819 MILWAUKEE, WI 53213

Visit Hal Leonard Online at
www.halleonard.com

Beautiful

Registration 2
Rhythm: Ballad

Words and Music by
Linda Perry

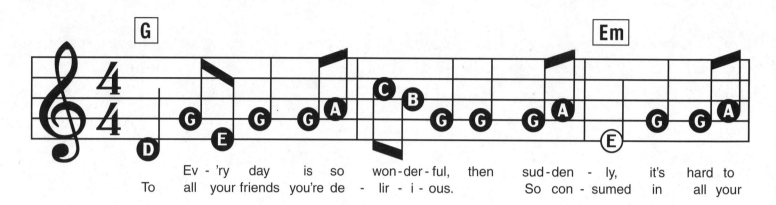

Ev - 'ry day is so won-der-ful, then sud-den - ly, it's hard to
To all your friends you're de - lir - i - ous. So con - sumed in all your

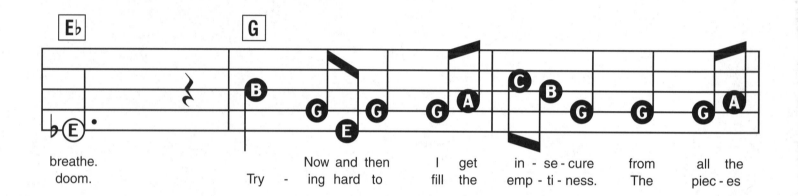

breathe. Now and then I get in - se - cure from all the
doom. Try - ing hard to fill the emp - ti - ness. The piec - es

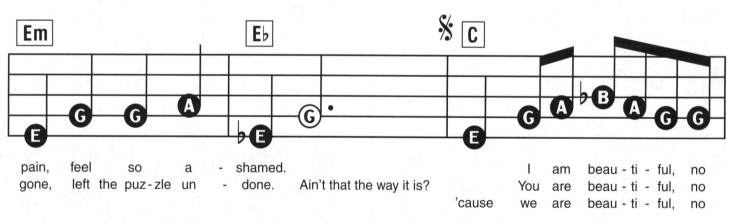

pain, feel so a - shamed. I am beau - ti - ful, no
gone, left the puz - zle un - done. Ain't that the way it is? You are beau - ti - ful, no
'cause we are beau - ti - ful, no

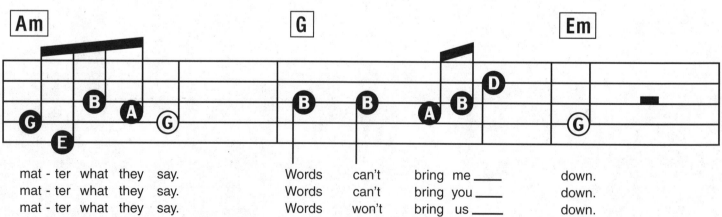

mat - ter what they say. Words can't bring me ___ down.
mat - ter what they say. Words can't bring you ___ down.
mat - ter what they say. Words won't bring us ___ down.

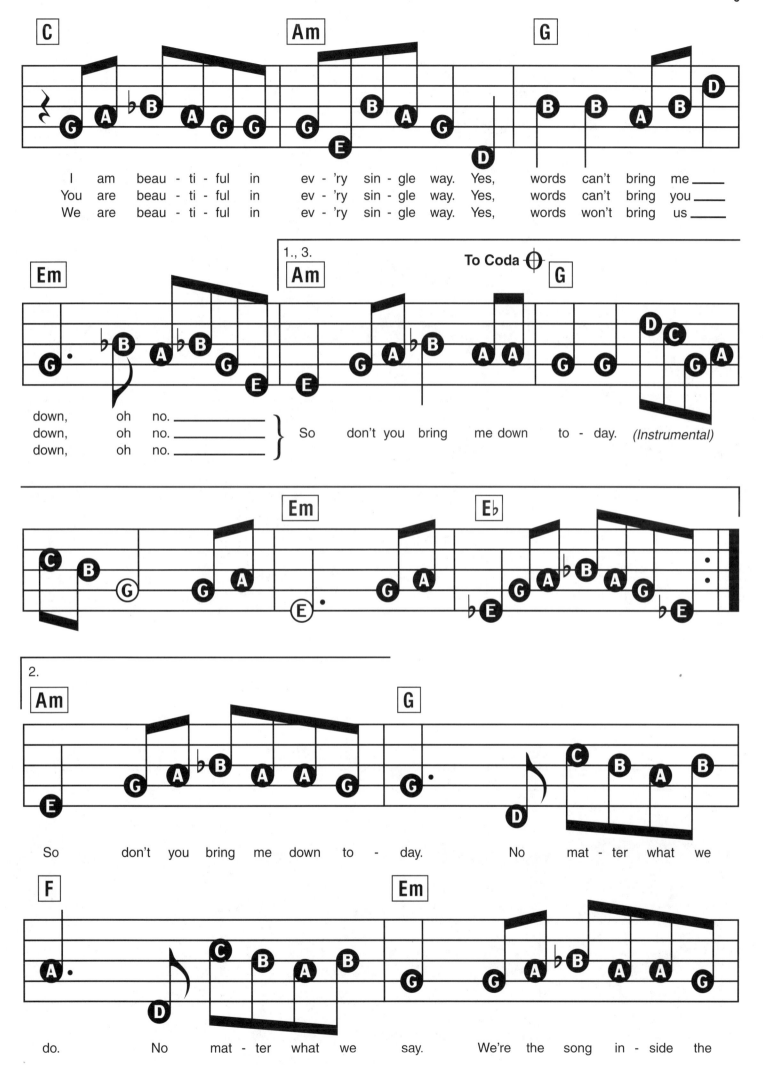

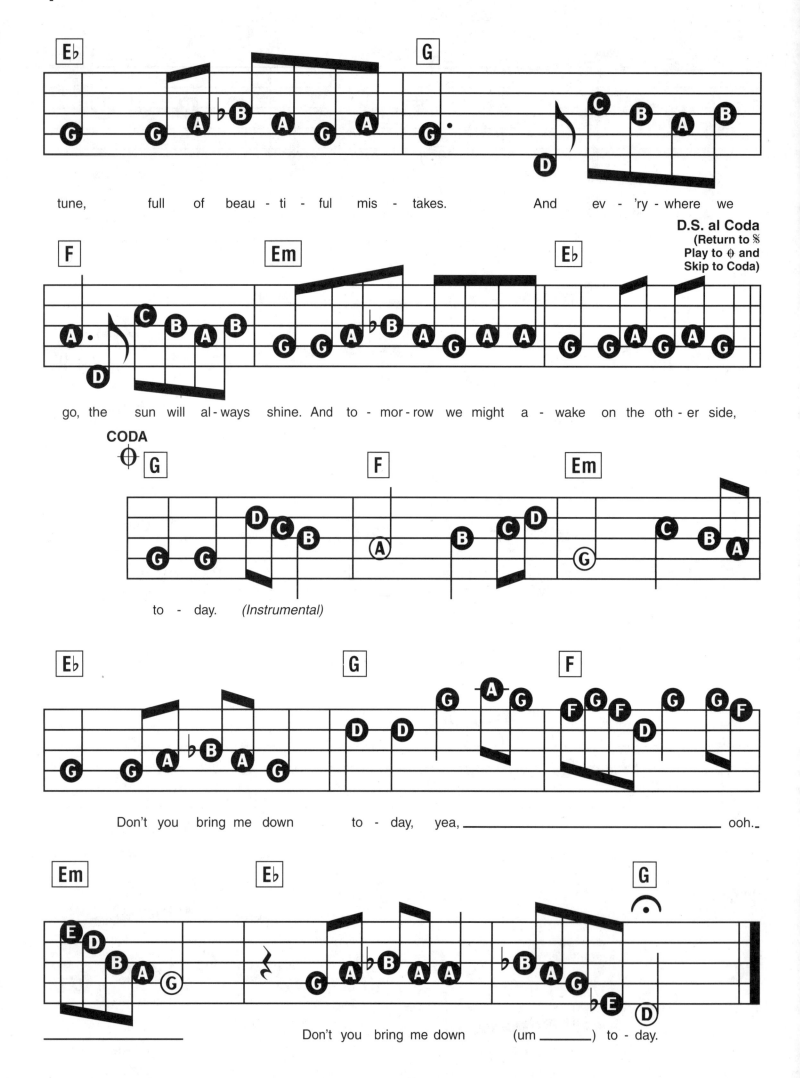

Bless the Broken Road

Registration 1
Rhythm: Country Rock or Rock

Words and Music by Marcus Hummon,
Bobby Boyd and Jeff Hanna

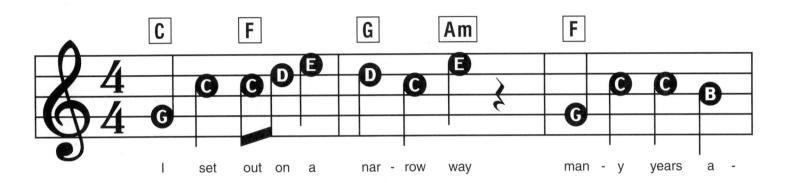

I set out on a nar - row way man - y years a -

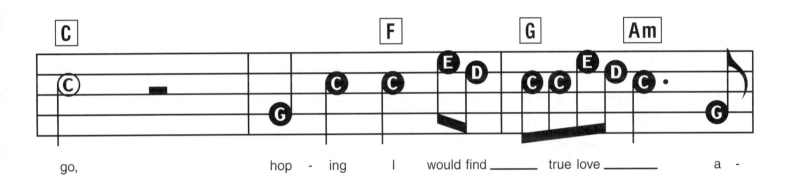

go, hop - ing I would find _____ true love _____ a -

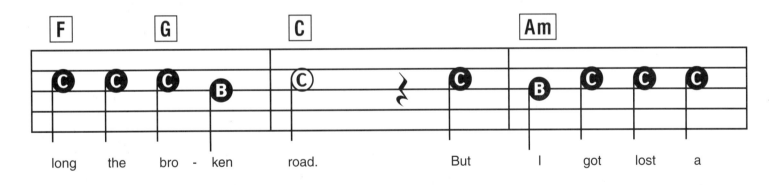

long the bro - ken road. But I got lost a

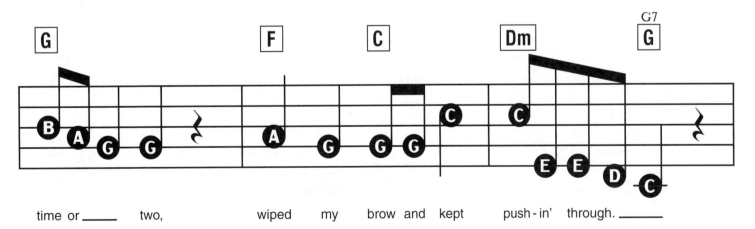

time or _____ two, wiped my brow and kept push - in' through. _____

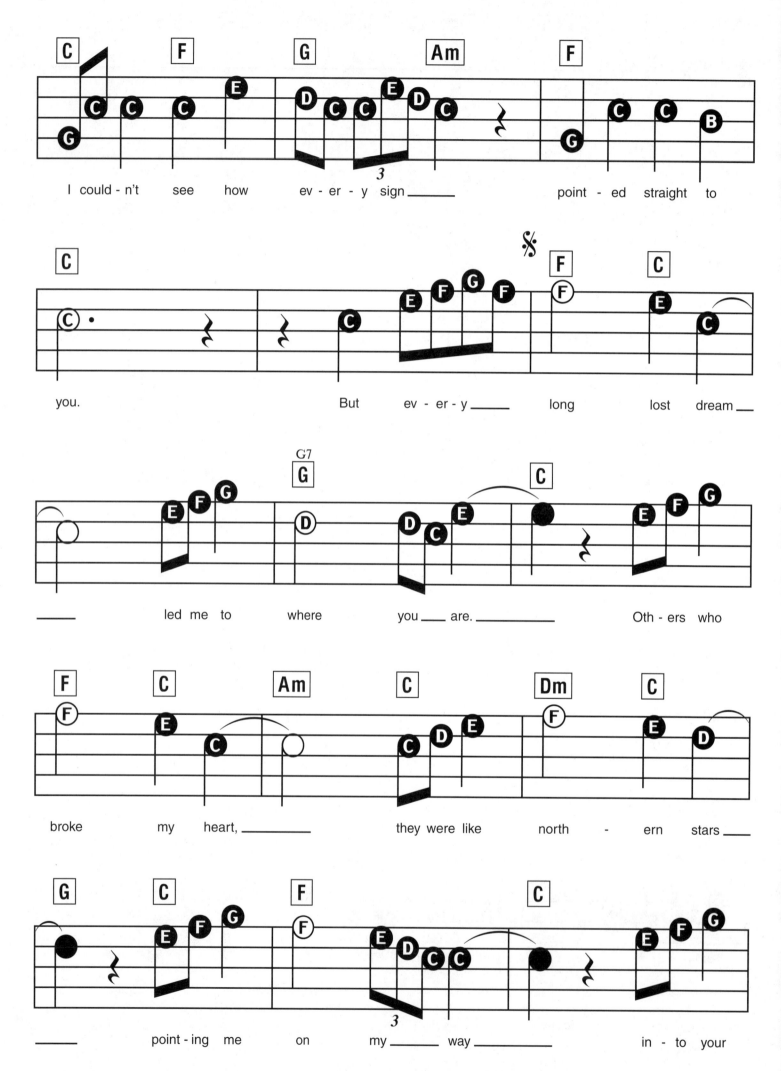

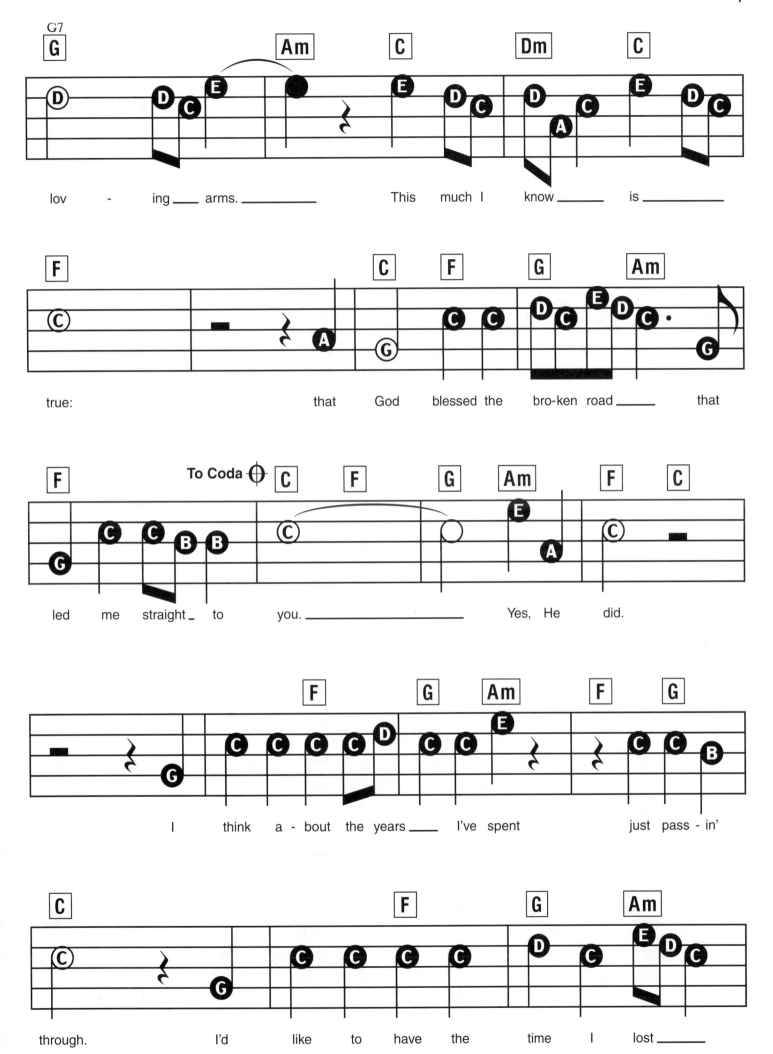

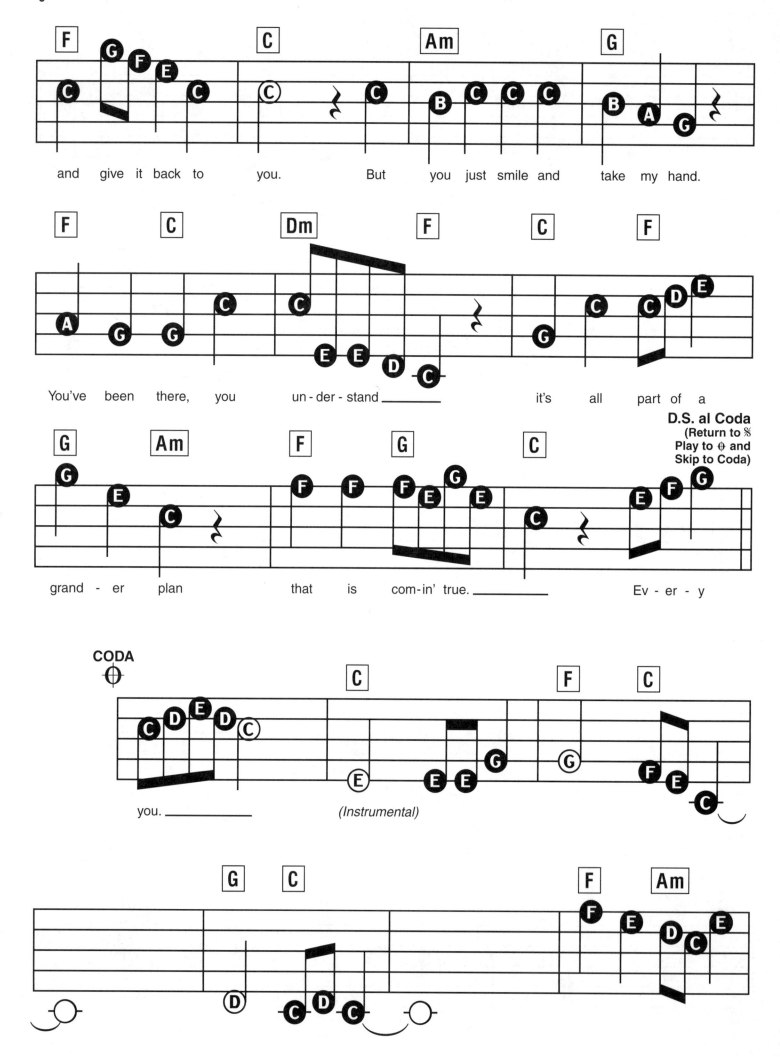

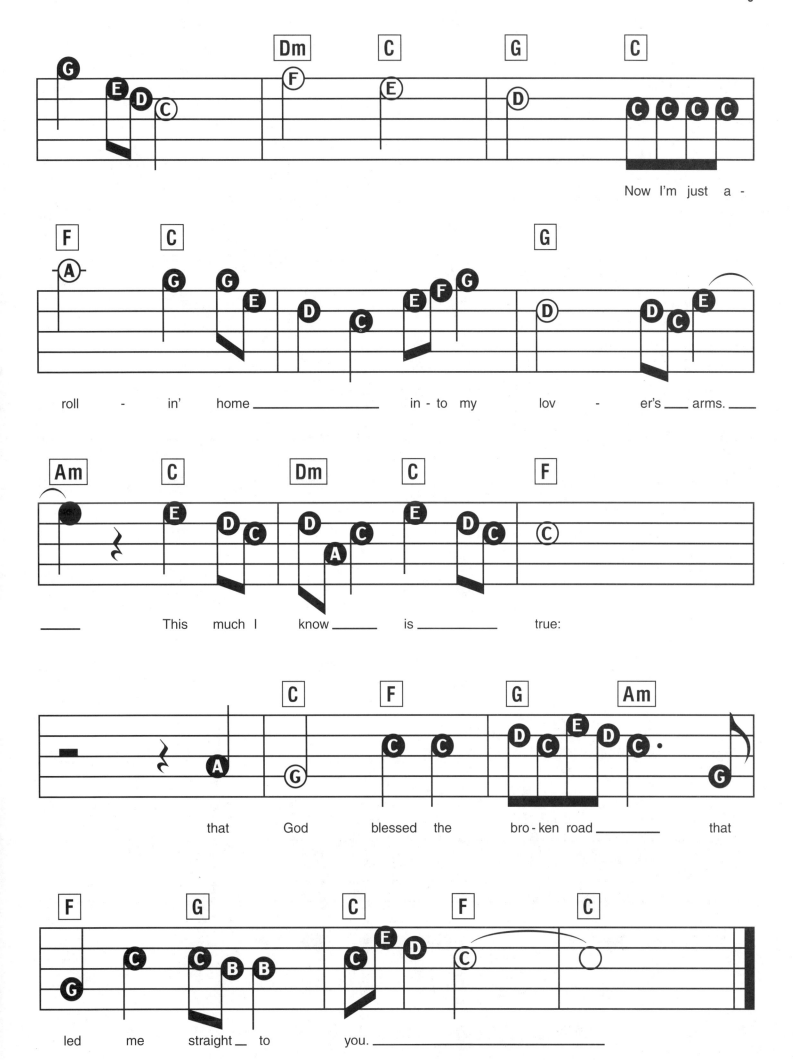

9

Breakaway

from THE PRINCESS DIARIES 2: ROYAL ENGAGEMENT

Registration 8
Rhythm: Waltz

Words and Music by Bridget Benenate,
Avril Lavigne and Matthew Gerrard

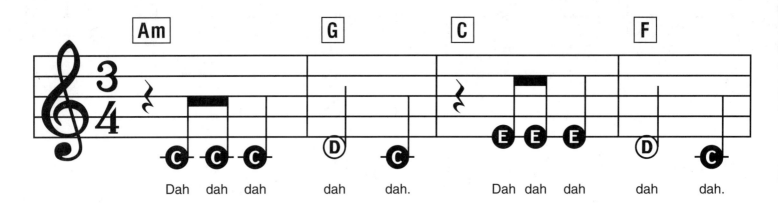

Dah dah dah   dah dah.   Dah dah dah   dah dah.

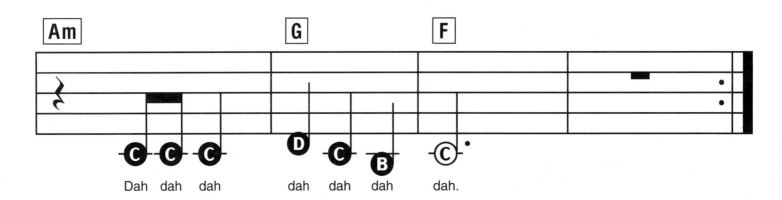

Dah dah dah   dah dah dah   dah.

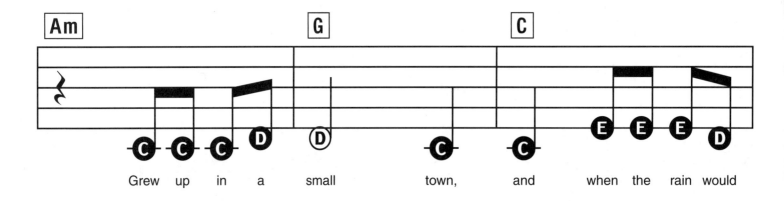

Grew up in a   small   town,   and   when the rain would

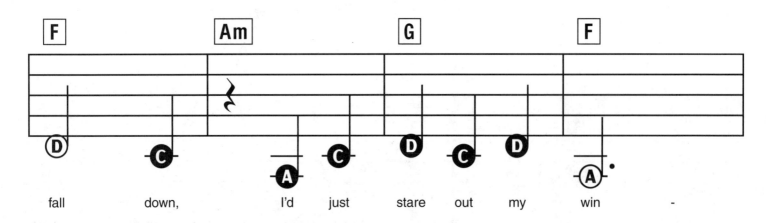

fall   down,   I'd   just   stare out my   win -

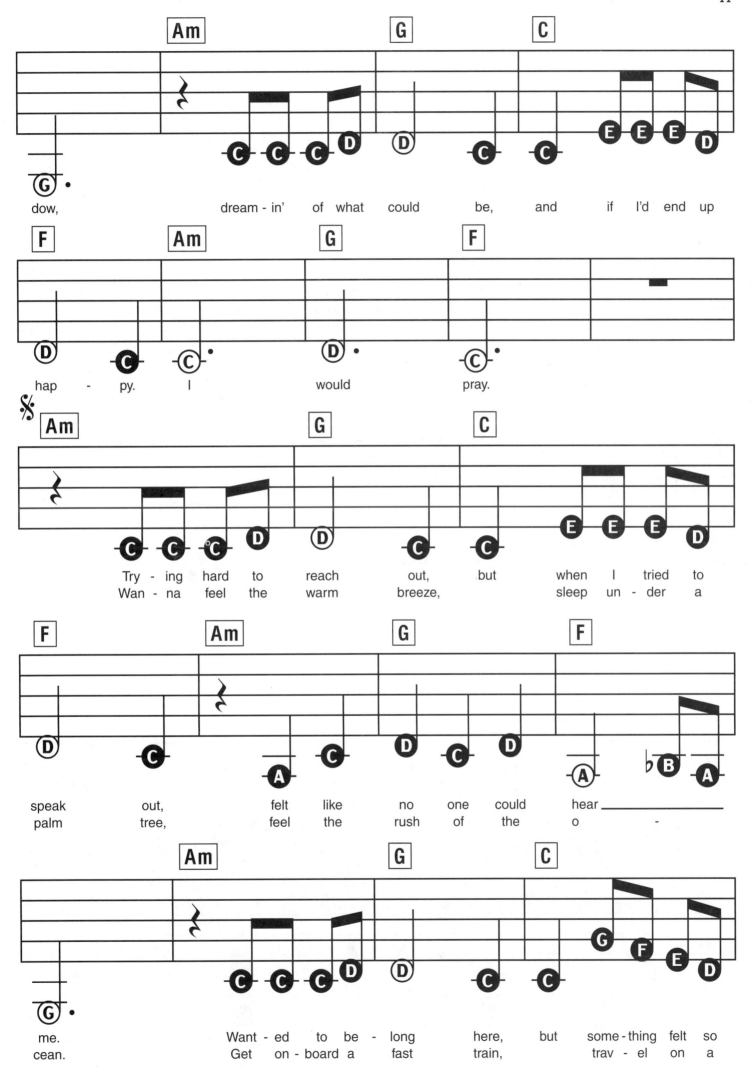

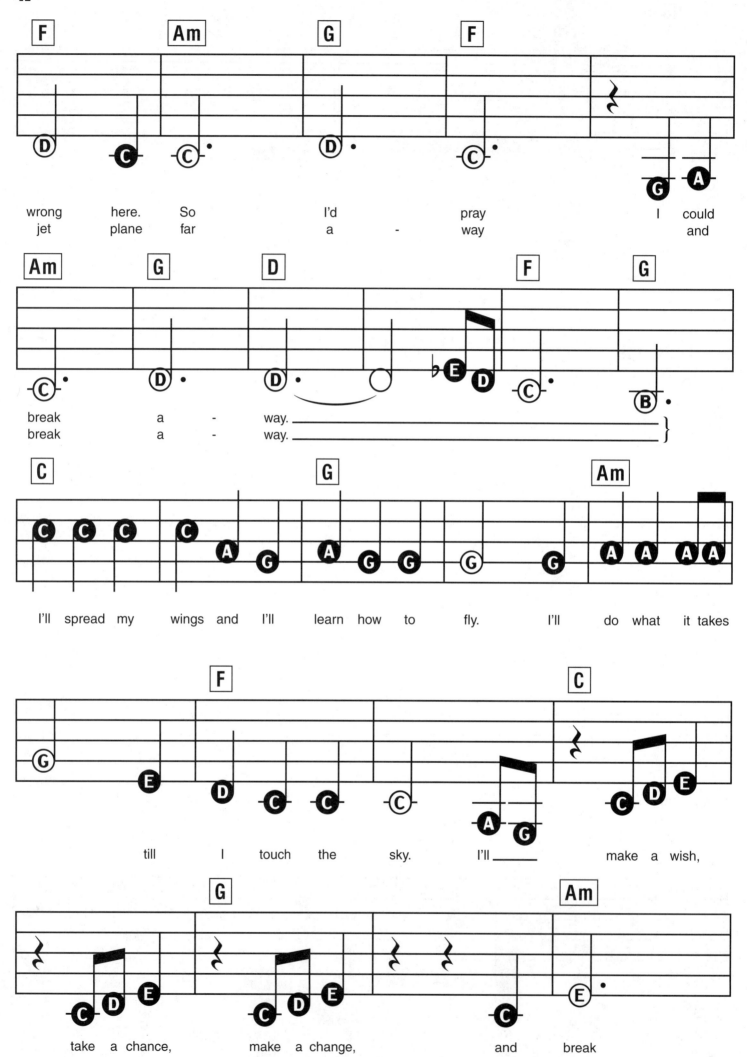

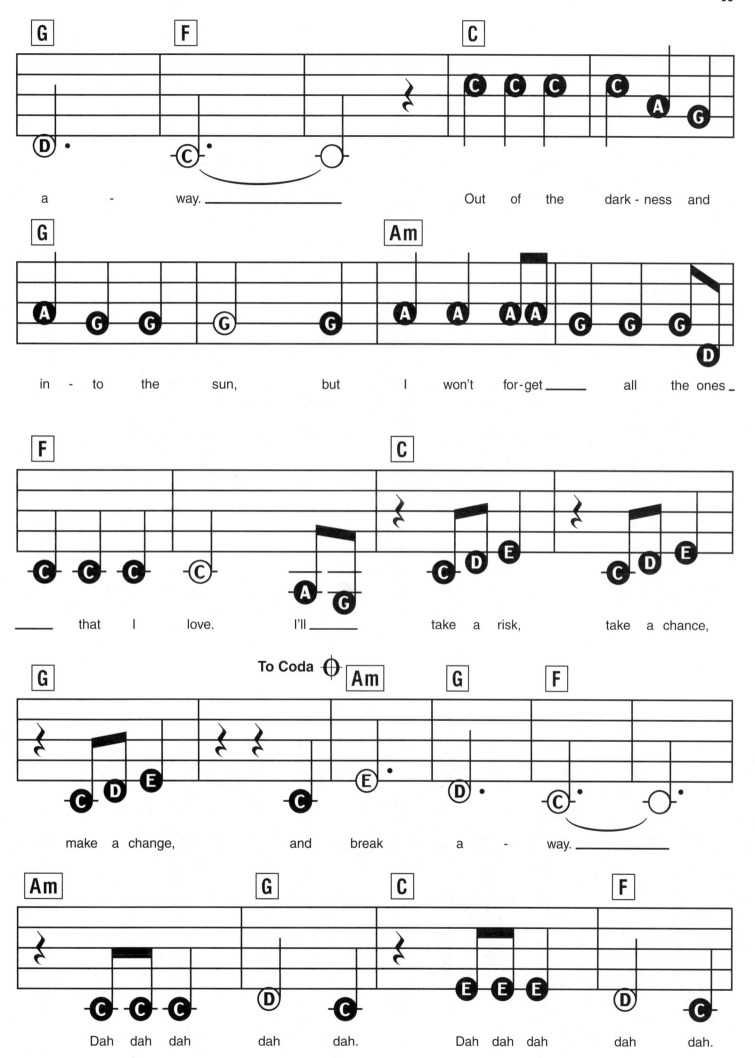

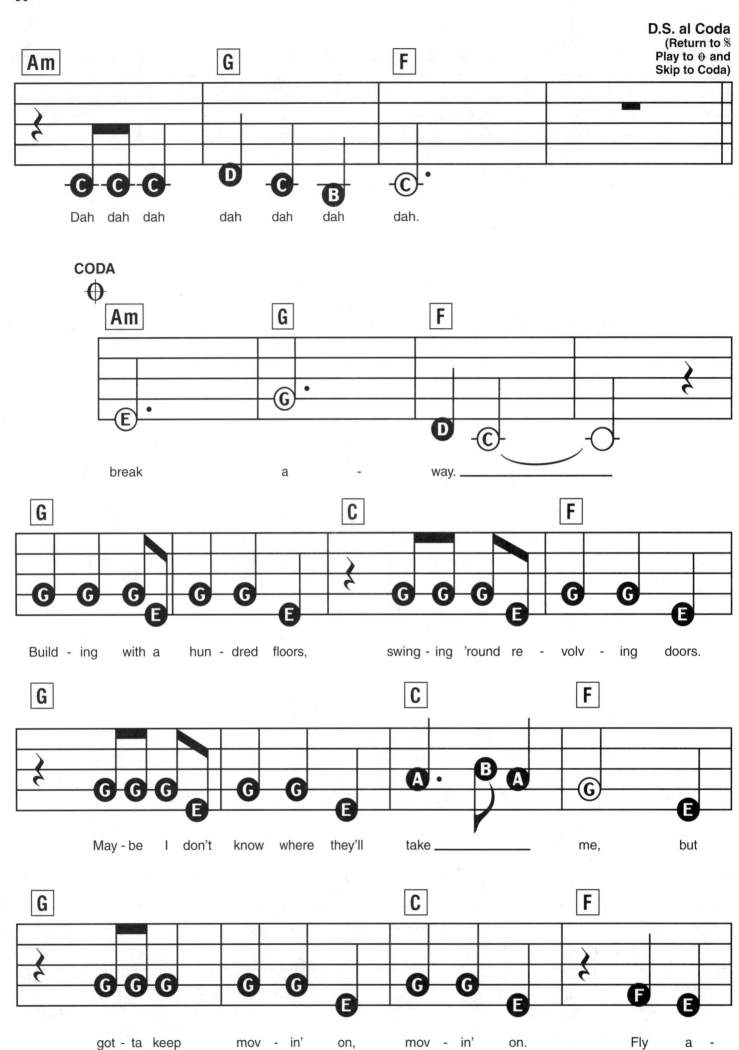

D.S. al Coda
(Return to %
Play to ⊕ and
Skip to Coda)

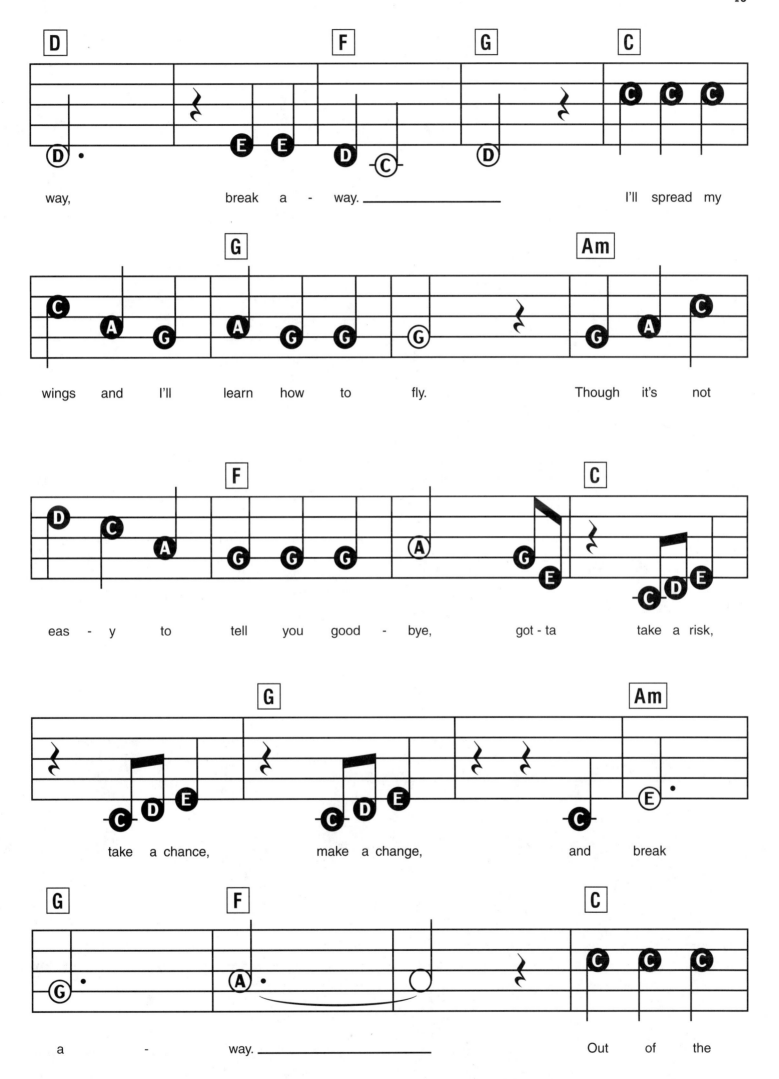

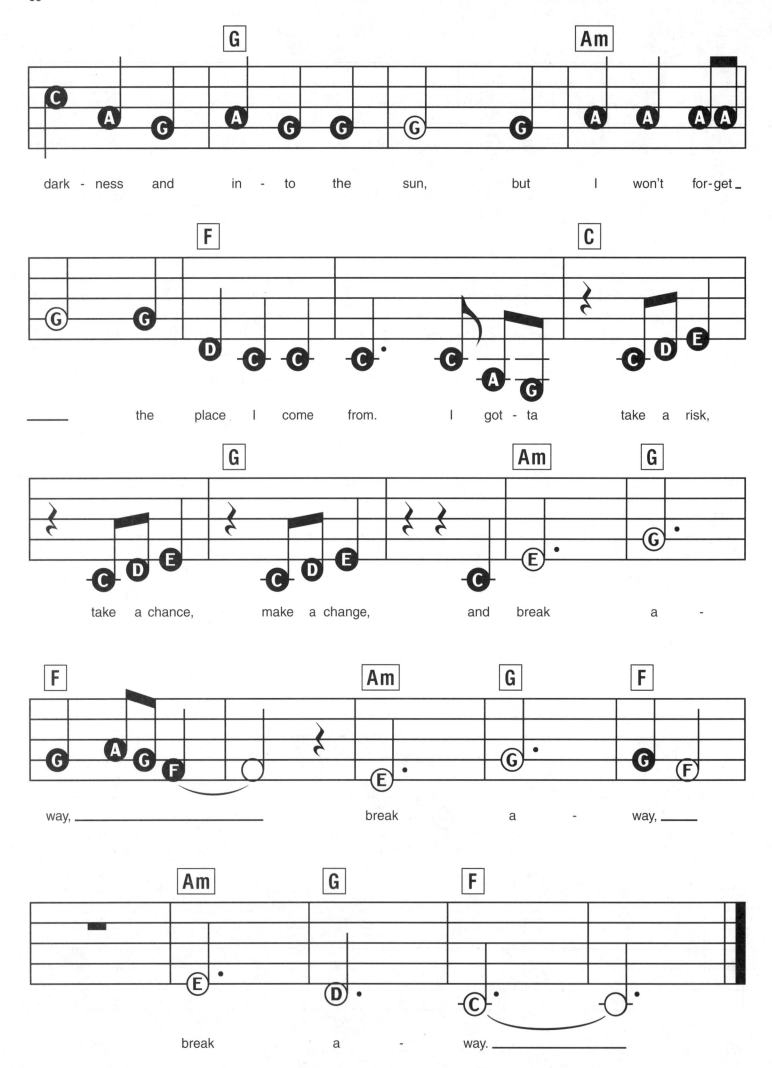

Breathe

Registration 7
Rhythm: Country Pop or Ballad

Words and Music by Holly Lamar
and Stephanie Bentley

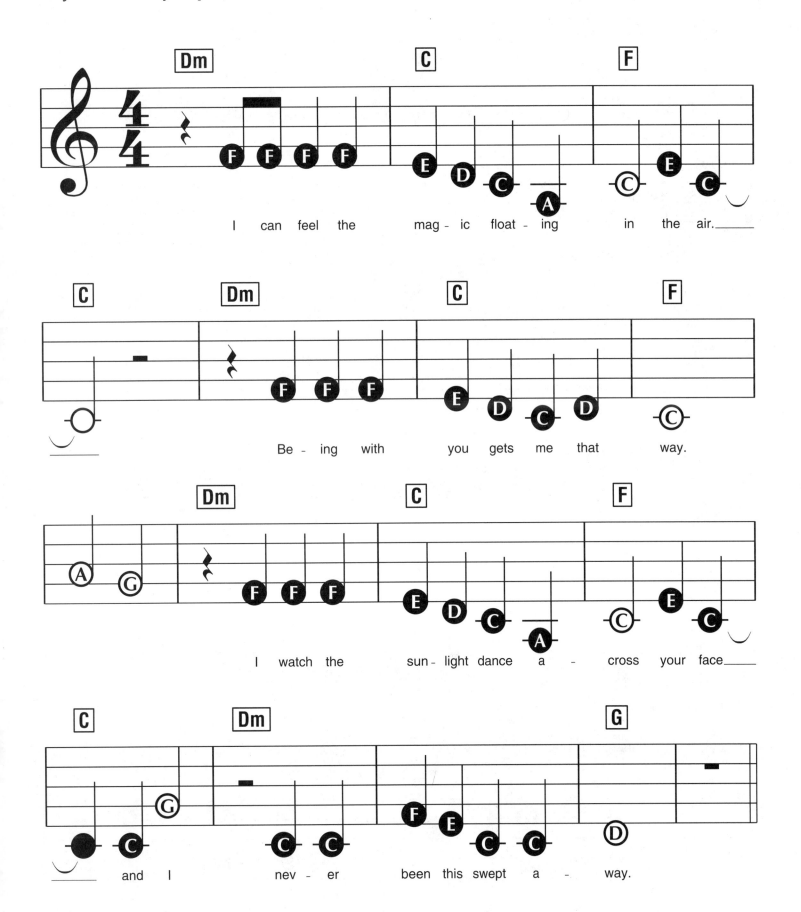

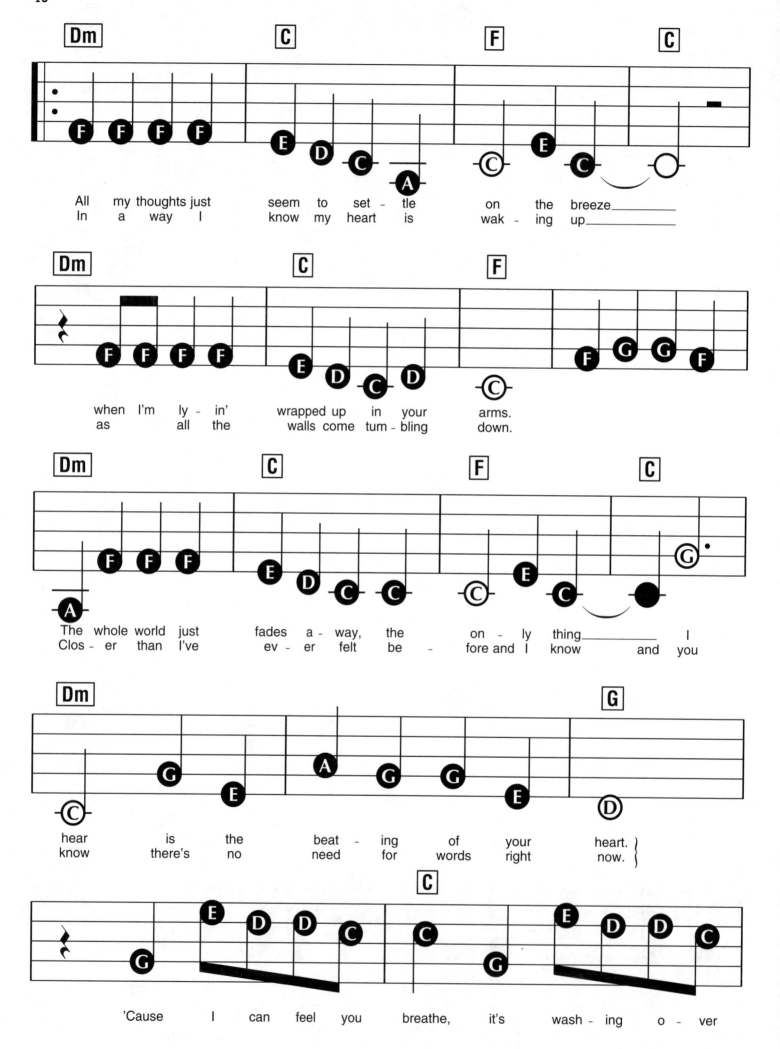

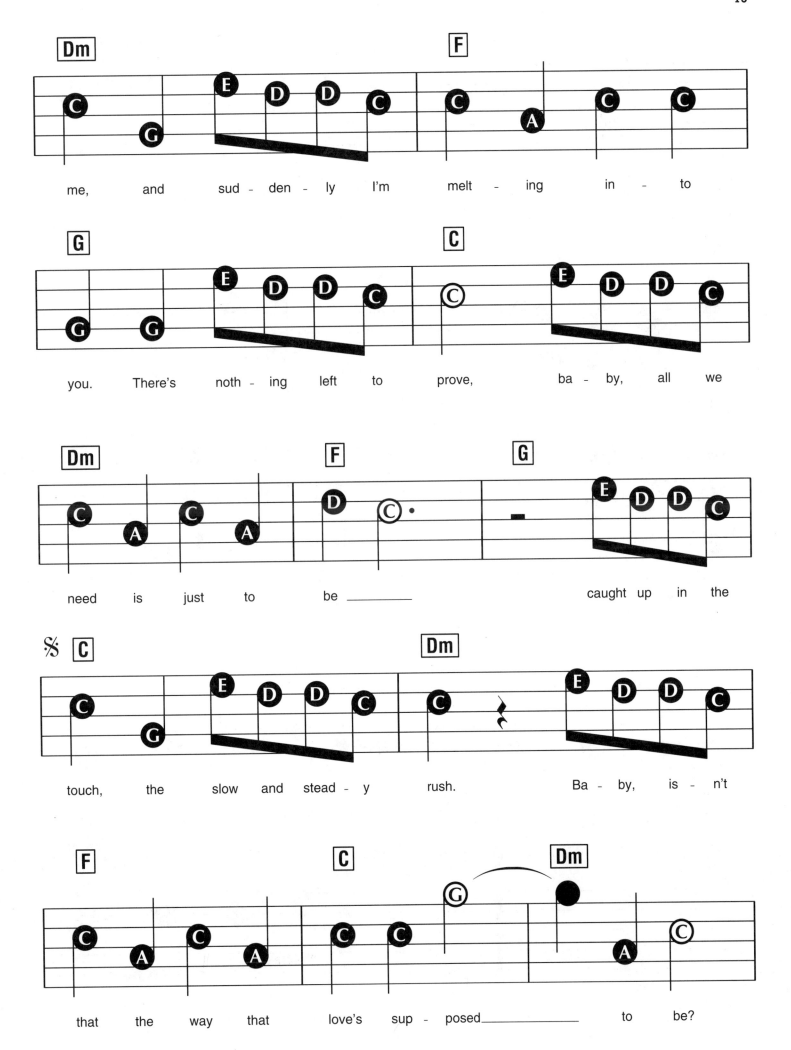

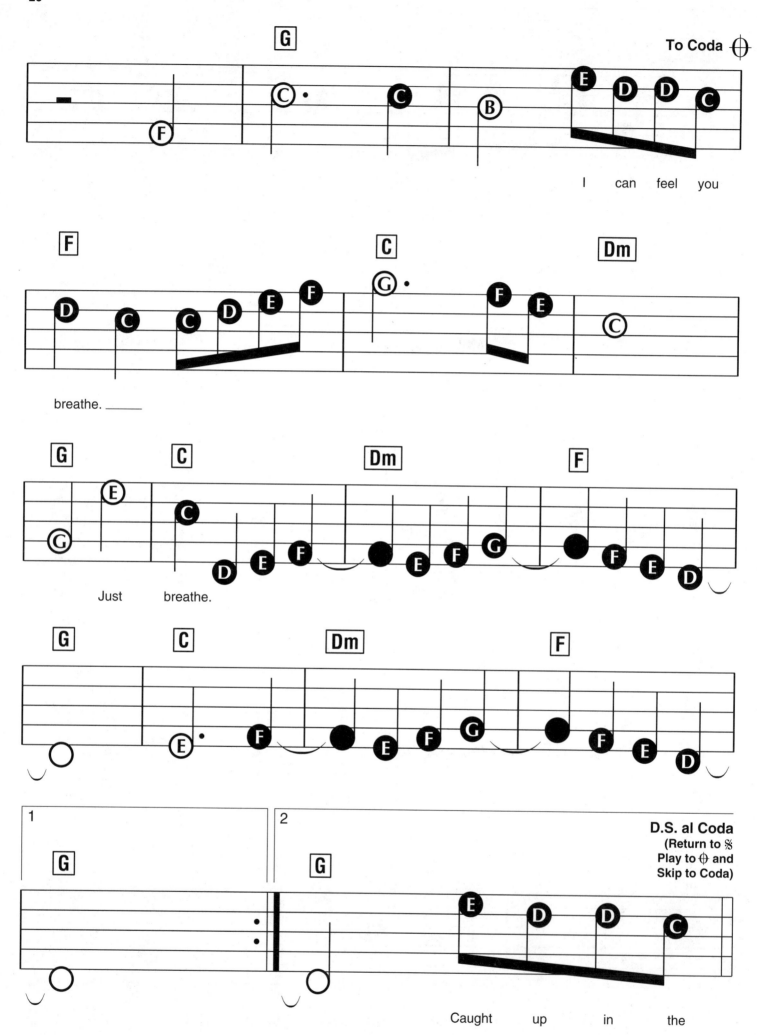

I can feel you

breathe. _____

Just breathe.

D.S. al Coda
(Return to %
Play to and
Skip to Coda)

Caught up in the

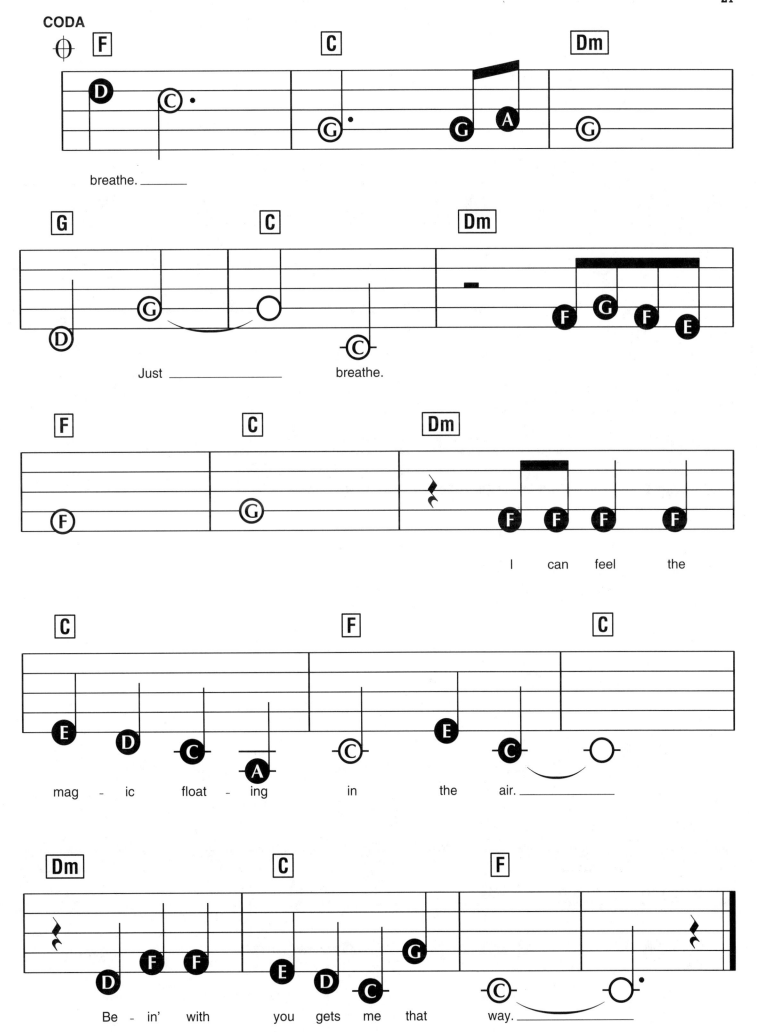

Don't Know Why

Registration 8
Rhythm: 8-Beat or Bossa Nova

Words and Music by
Jesse Harris

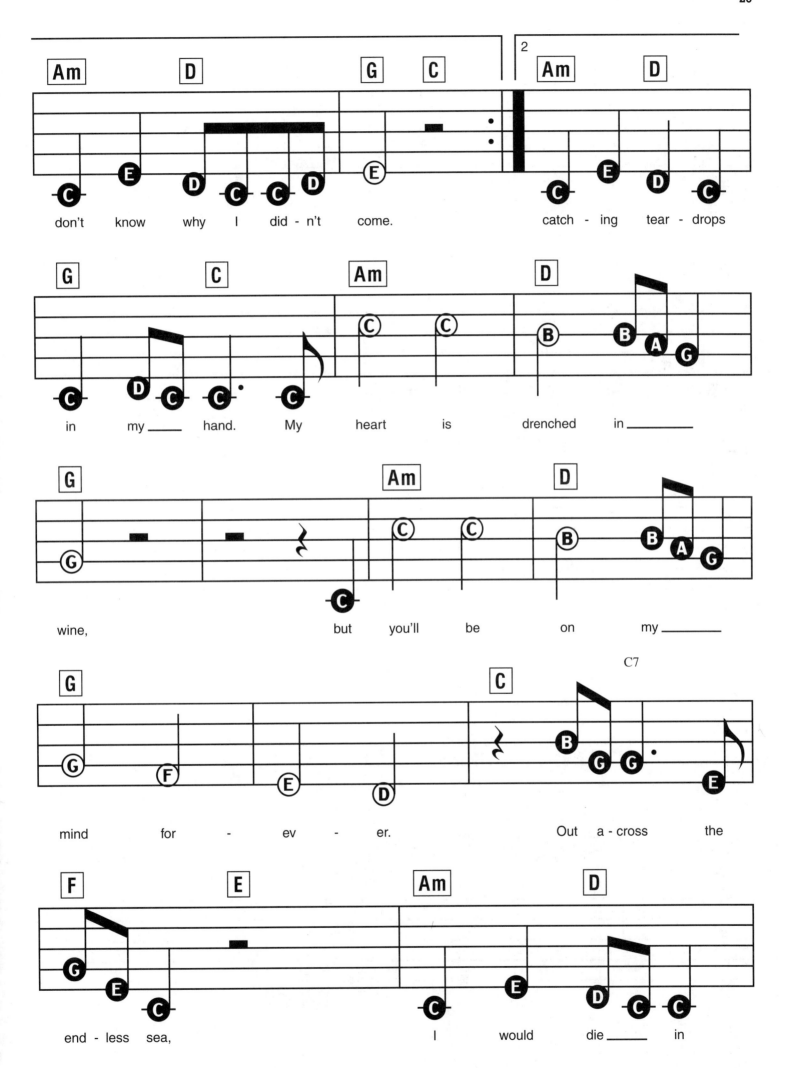

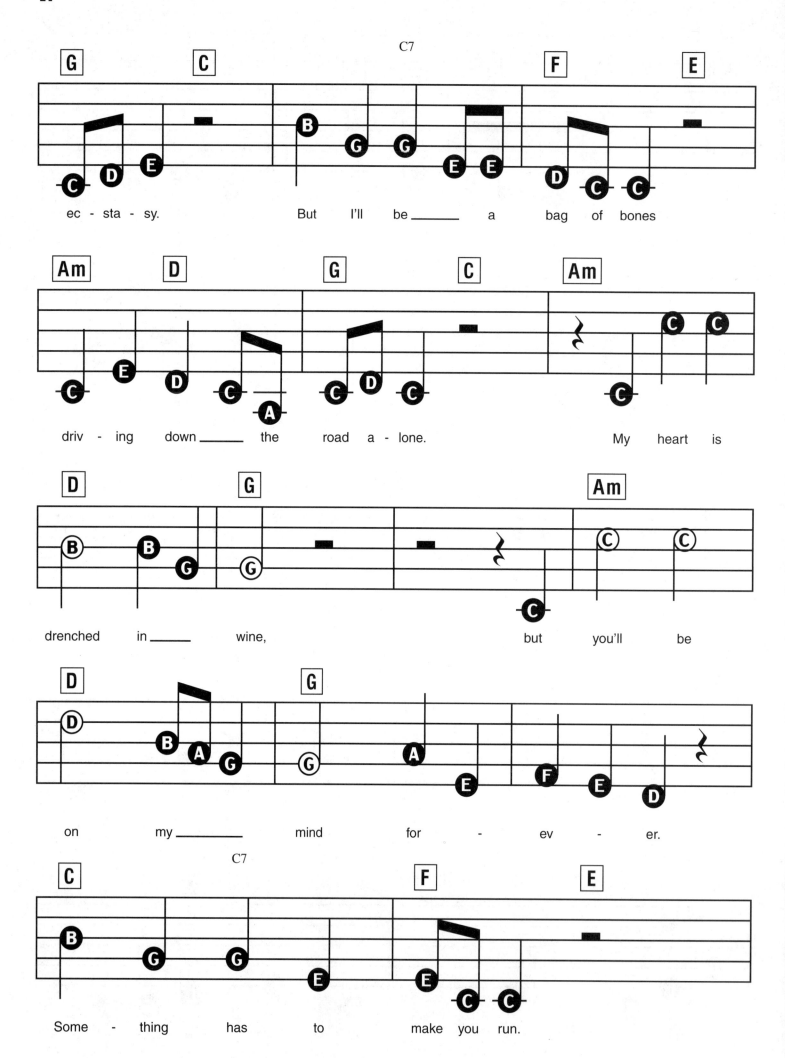

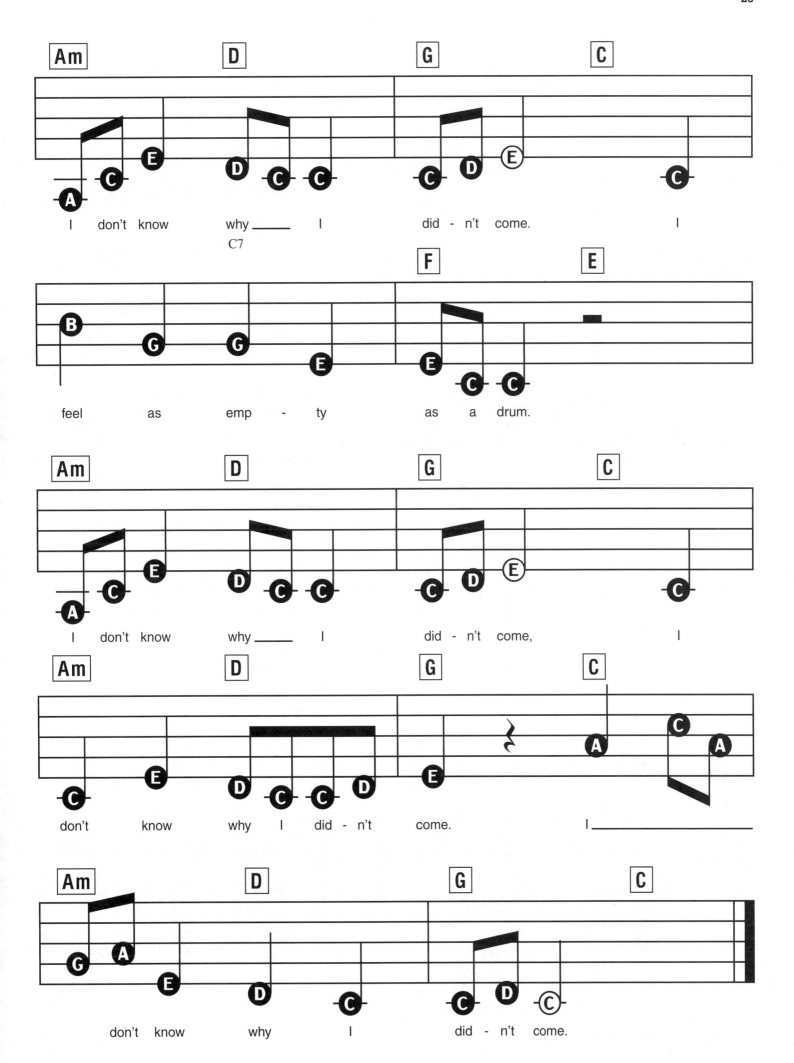

Dust in the Wind

Words and Music by
Kerry Livgren

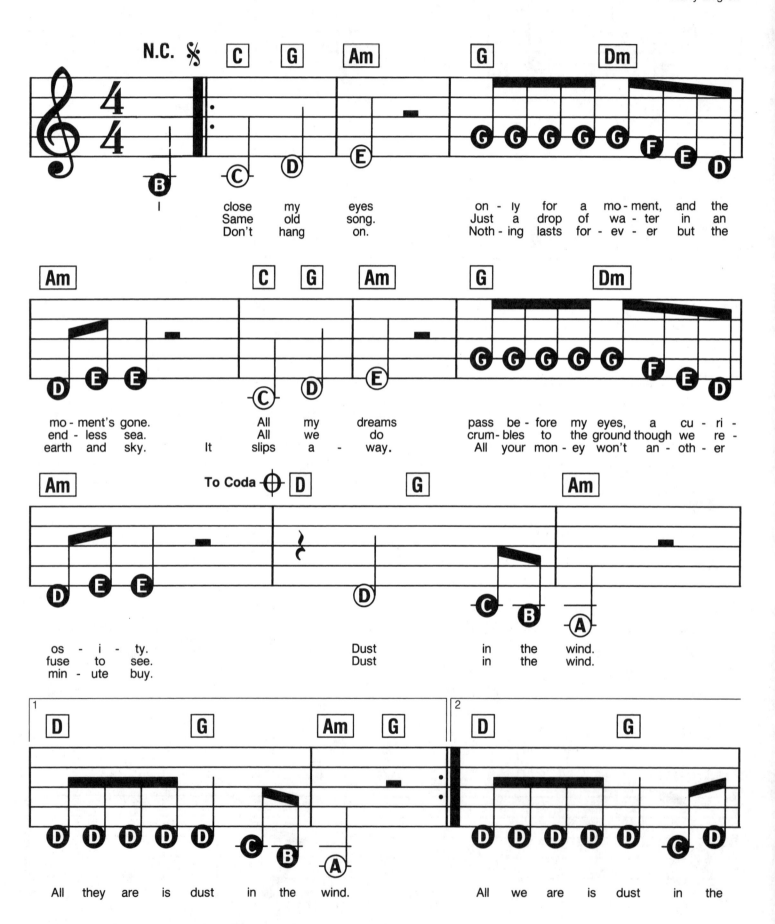

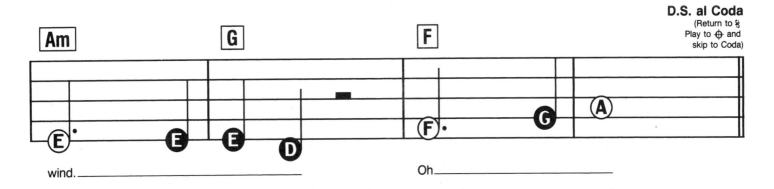

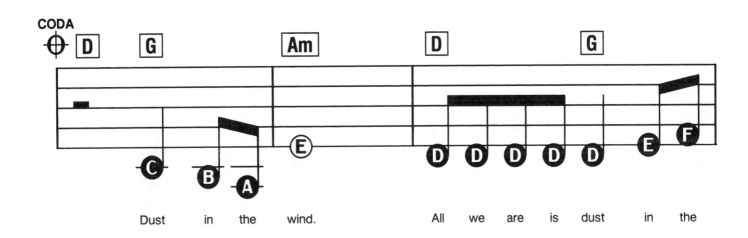

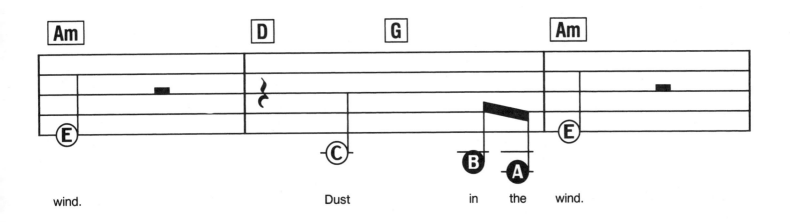

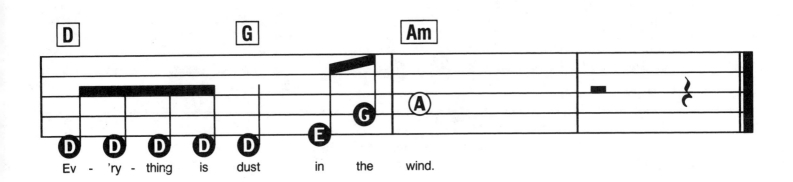

Every Breath You Take

Registration 1
Rhythm: Rock or 8 Beat

Music and Lyrics by
Sting

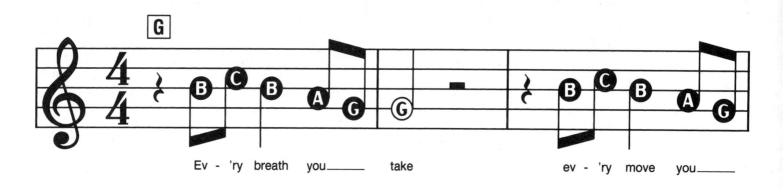

Ev - 'ry breath you___ take   ev - 'ry move you___

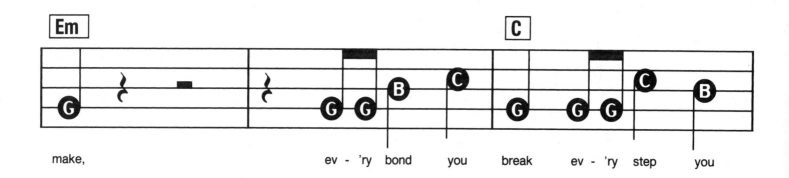

make,   ev - 'ry bond you break   ev - 'ry step you

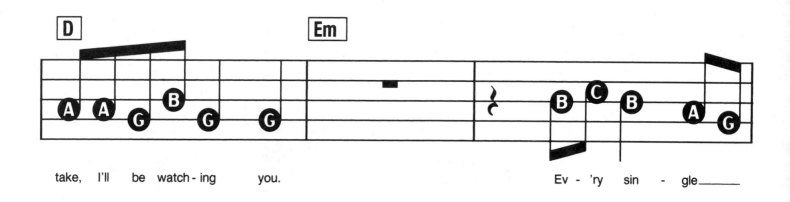

take, I'll be watch - ing you.   Ev - 'ry sin - gle___

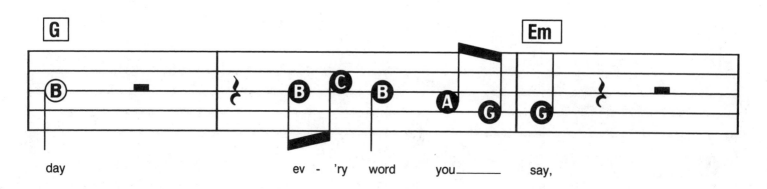

day   ev - 'ry word you___ say,

29

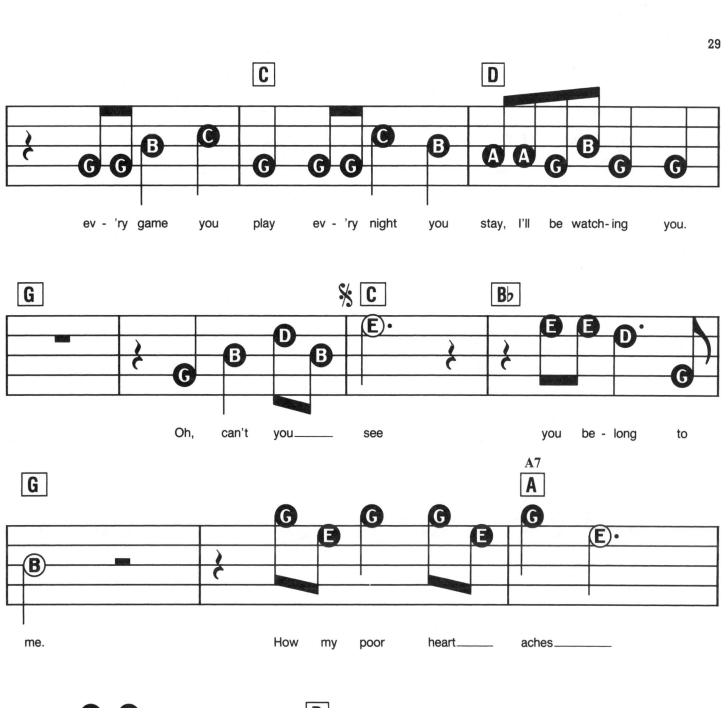

ev - 'ry game you play ev - 'ry night you stay, I'll be watch-ing you.

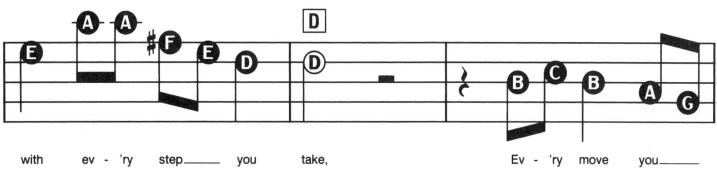

Oh, can't you___ see you be - long to

me. How my poor heart___ aches___

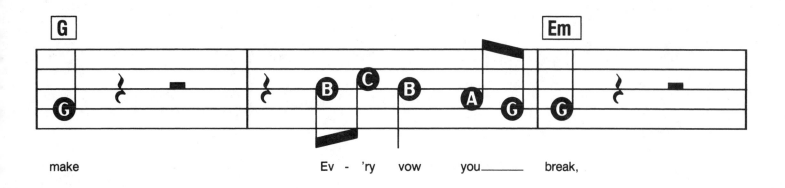

with ev - 'ry step___ you take, Ev - 'ry move you___

make Ev - 'ry vow you___ break,

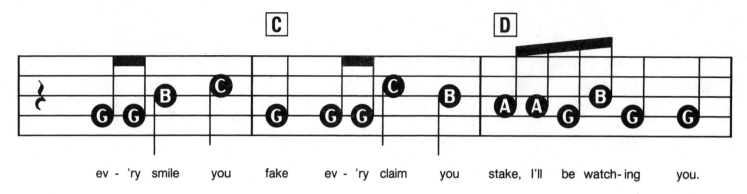

ev - 'ry smile you fake ev - 'ry claim you stake, I'll be watch- ing you.

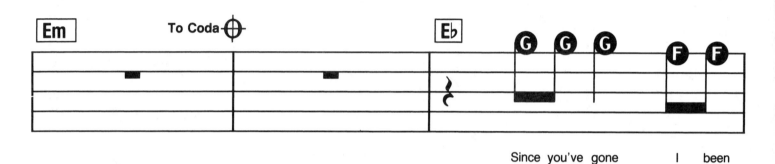

Since you've gone I been

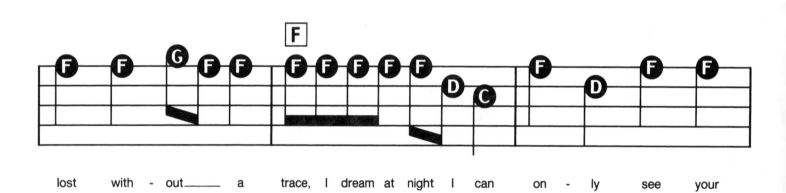

lost with - out_____ a trace, I dream at night I can on - ly see your

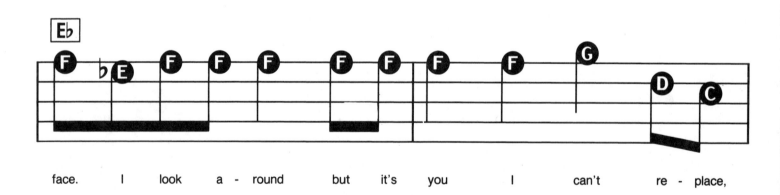

face. I look a - round but it's you I can't re - place,

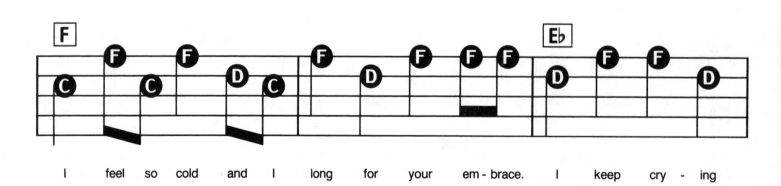

I feel so cold and I long for your em - brace. I keep cry - ing

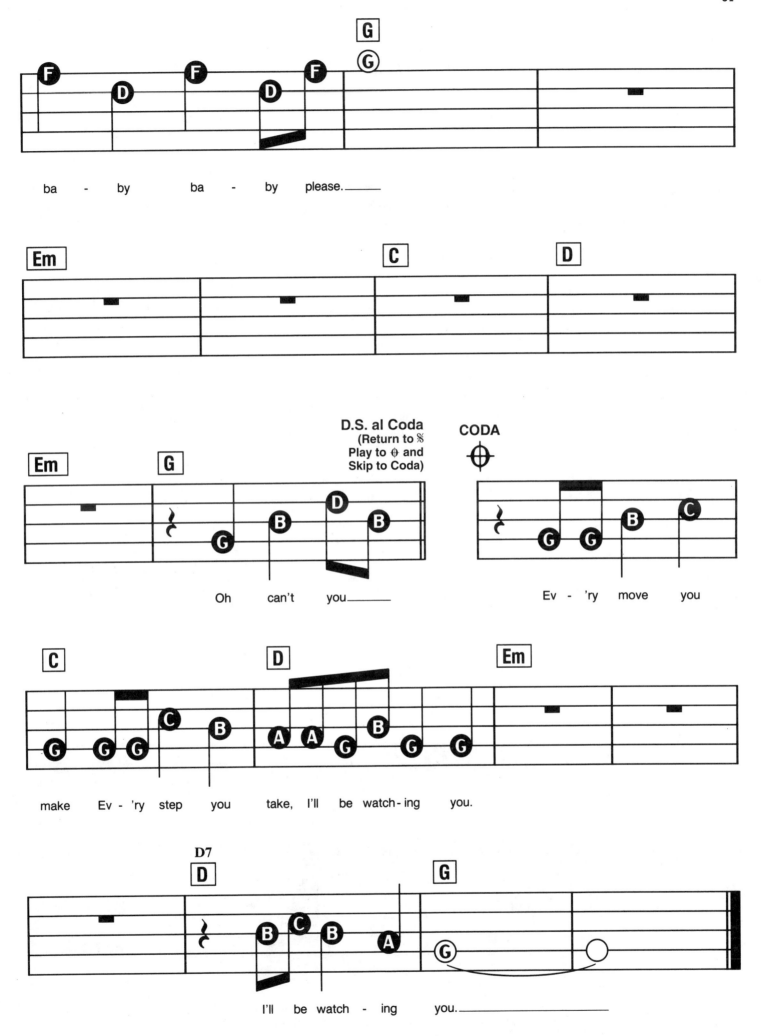

ba - by   ba - by   please._____

D.S. al Coda
(Return to 𝄋
Play to ⊕ and
Skip to Coda)

CODA

Oh   can't   you_____

Ev - 'ry   move   you

make   Ev - 'ry   step   you   take,   I'll   be   watch - ing   you.

I'll   be   watch - ing   you._____

(Everything I Do)
I Do It for You
from the Motion Picture ROBIN HOOD: PRINCE OF THIEVES

Registration 8
Rhythm: Rock or 8-Beat

Words and Music by Bryan Adams,
Robert John "Mutt" Lange and Michael Kamen

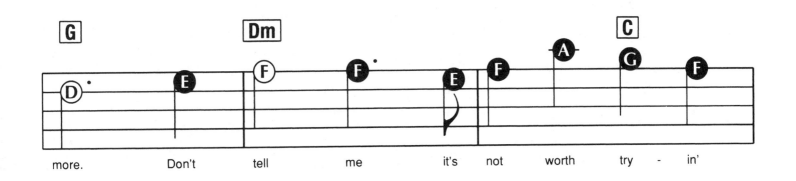

more. Don't tell me it's not worth try - in'

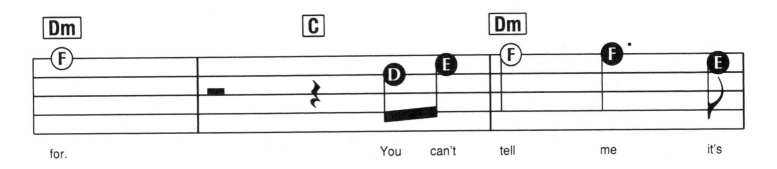

for. You can't tell me it's

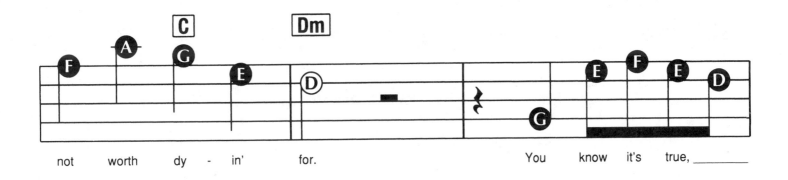

not worth dy - in' for. You know it's true, _____

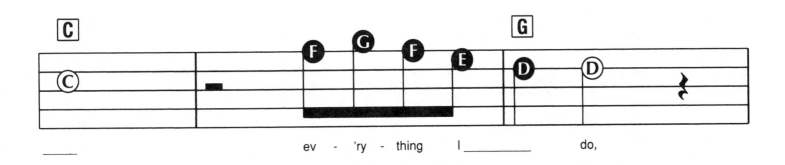

_____ ev - 'ry - thing I _____ do,

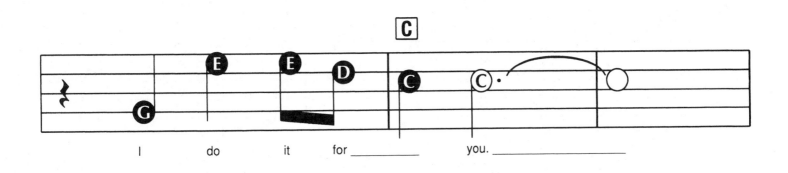

I do it for _____ you. _____

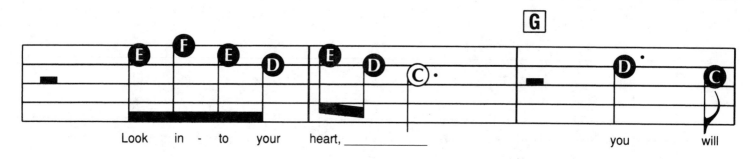

Look in - to your heart, _____ you will

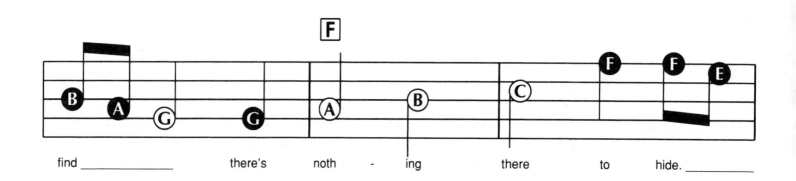

find _____ there's noth - ing there to hide. _____

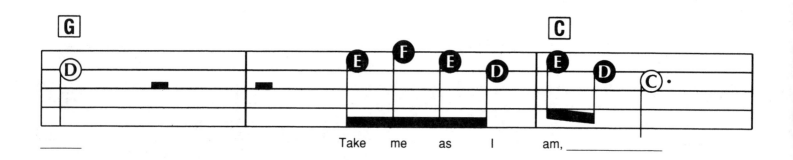

_____ Take me as I am, _____

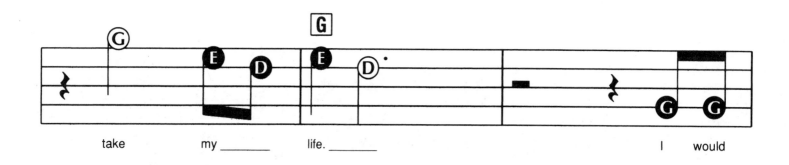

take my _____ life. _____ I would

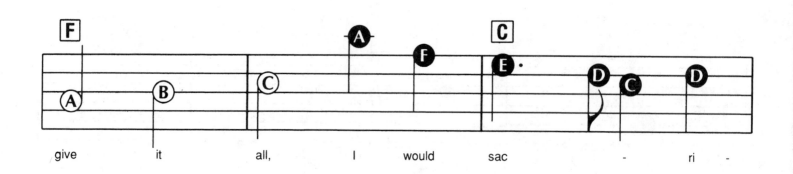

give it all, I would sac - ri -

35

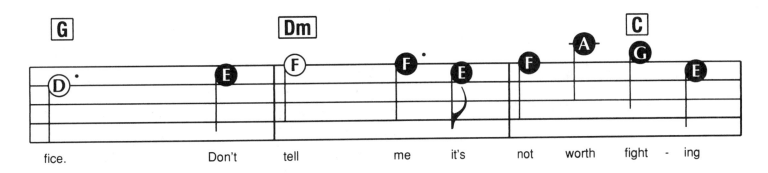

fice.   Don't tell me it's not worth fight - ing

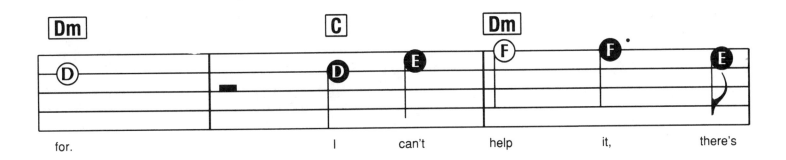

for.   I can't help it, there's

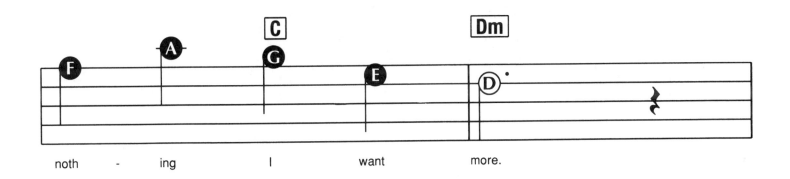

noth - ing I want more.

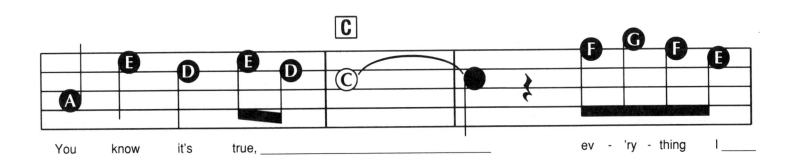

You know it's true,   ev - 'ry - thing I

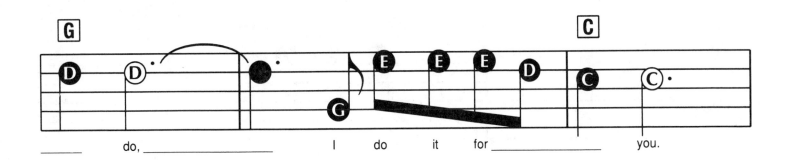

do,   I do it for you.

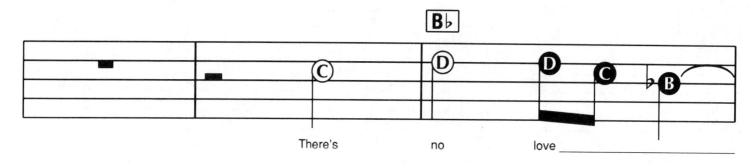

There's no love _____

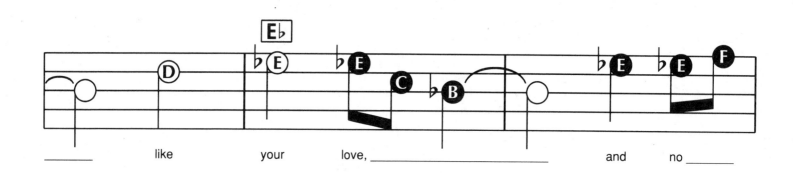

____ like your love, _____ and no _____

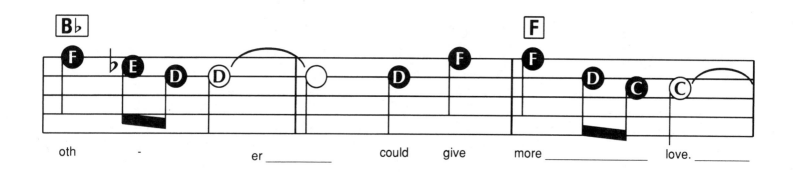

oth - er _____ could give more _____ love. _____

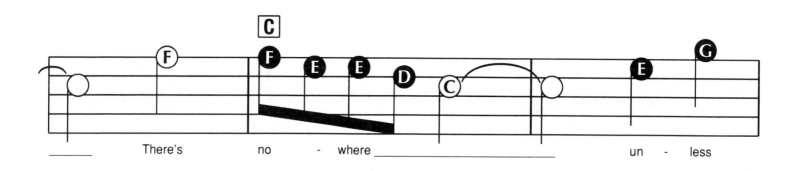

_____ There's no - where _____ un - less

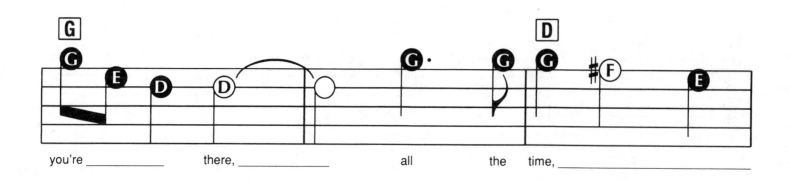

you're _____ there, _____ all the time, _____

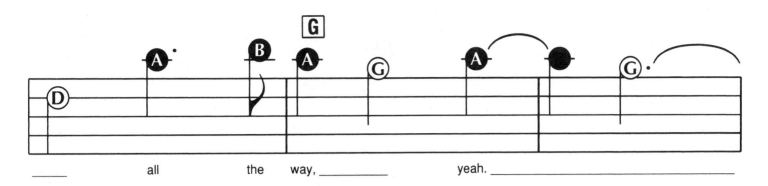

all   the   way, _____ yeah. _____

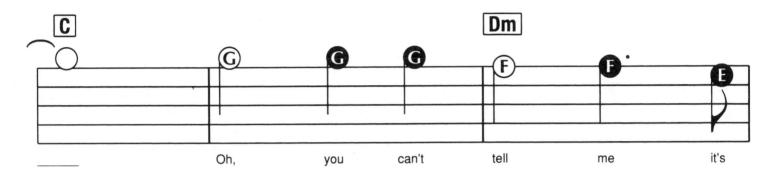

_____   Oh,   you   can't   tell   me   it's

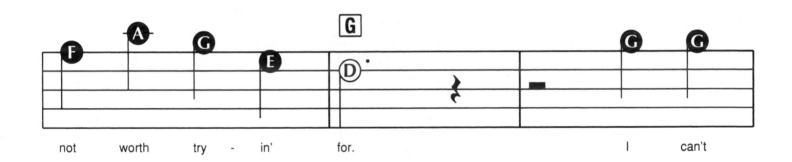

not   worth   try - in'   for.   I   can't

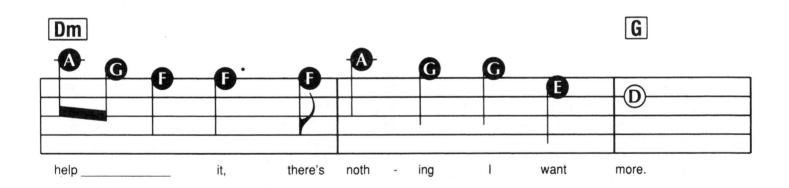

help _____ it,   there's   noth - ing   I   want   more.

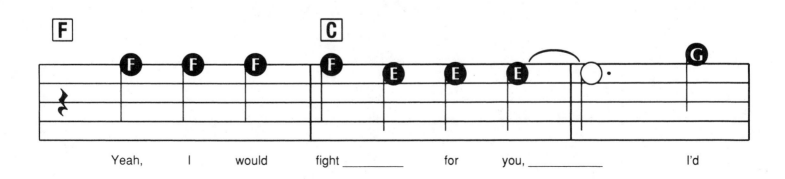

Yeah,   I   would   fight _____ for   you, _____ I'd

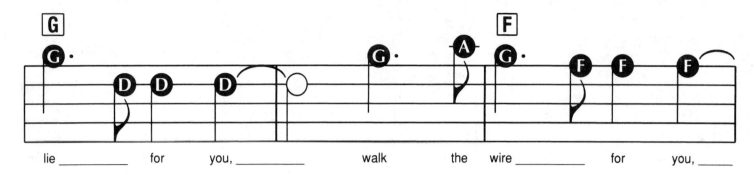

lie _____ for you, _____ walk the wire _____ for you, _____

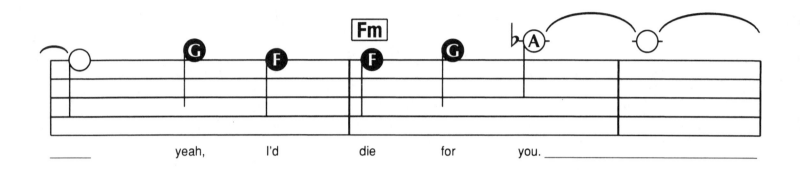

_____ yeah, I'd die for you. _____

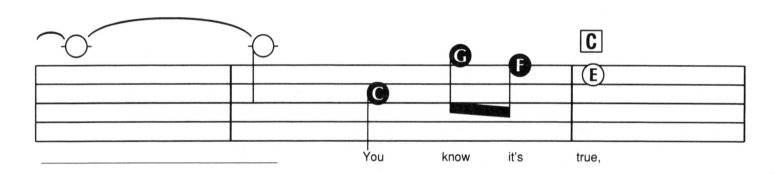

_____ You know it's true,

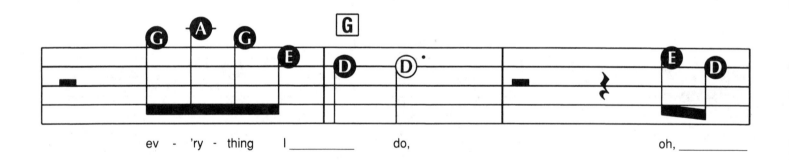

ev - 'ry - thing I _____ do, oh, _____

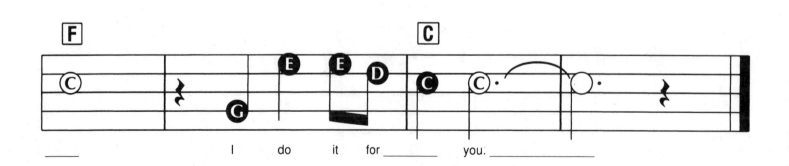

_____ I do it for _____ you. _____

Fallin'

Registration 8
Rhythm: Slow Rock

Words and Music by
Alicia Keys

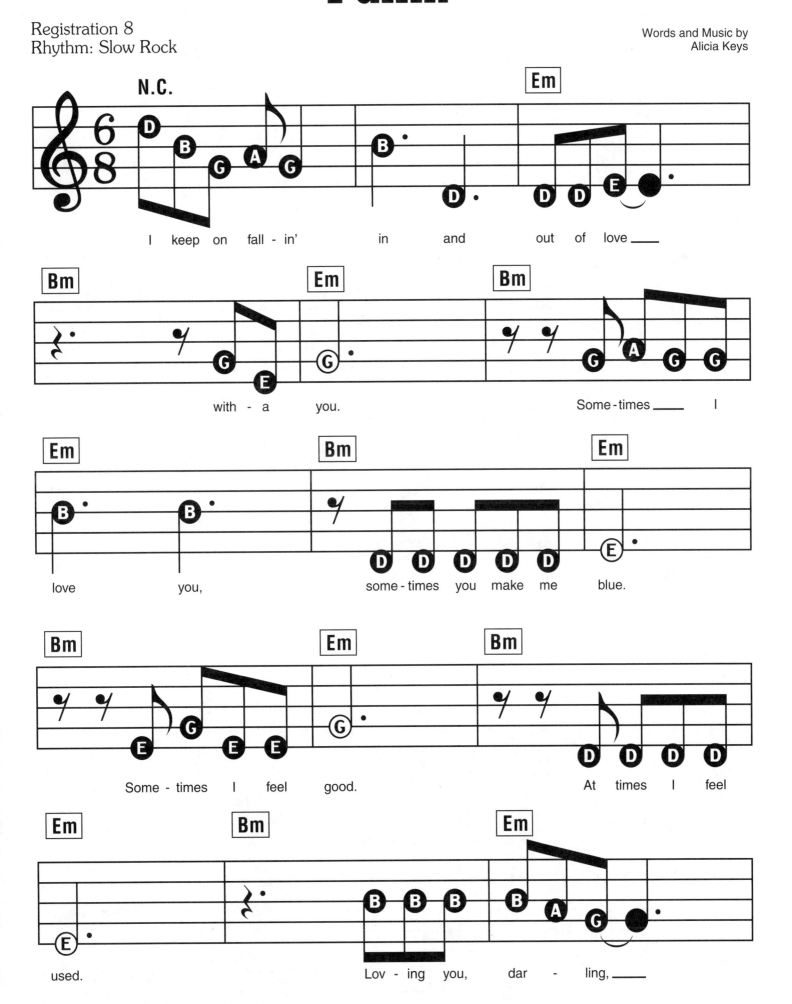

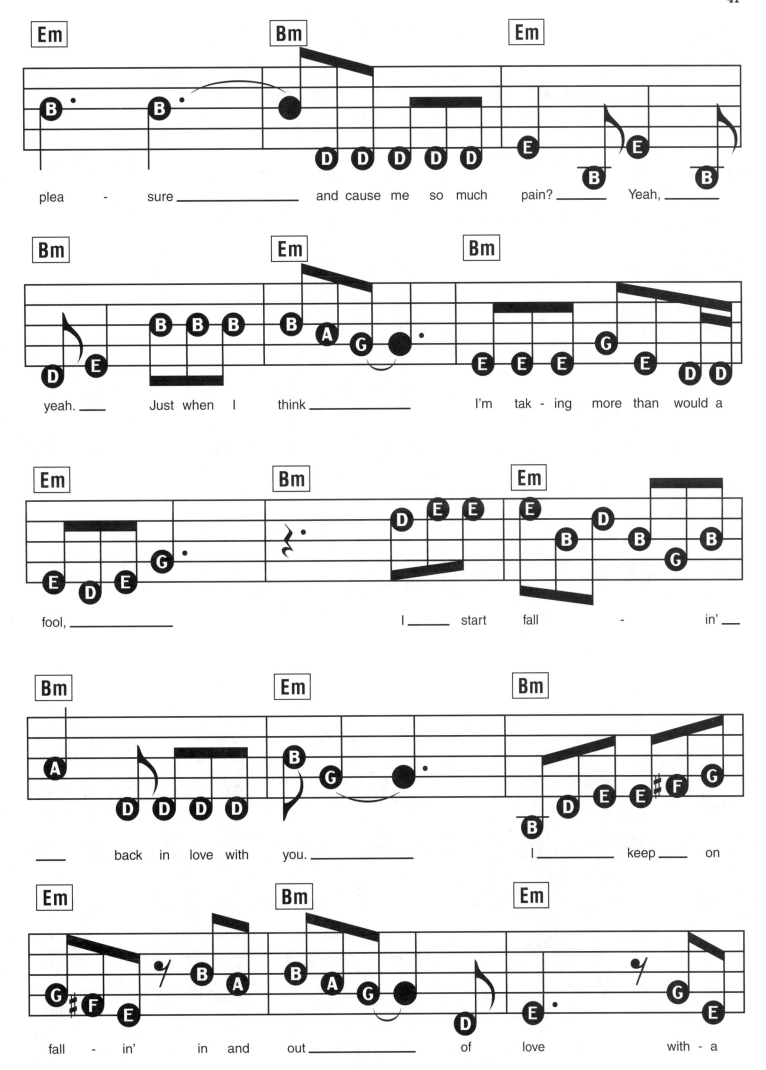

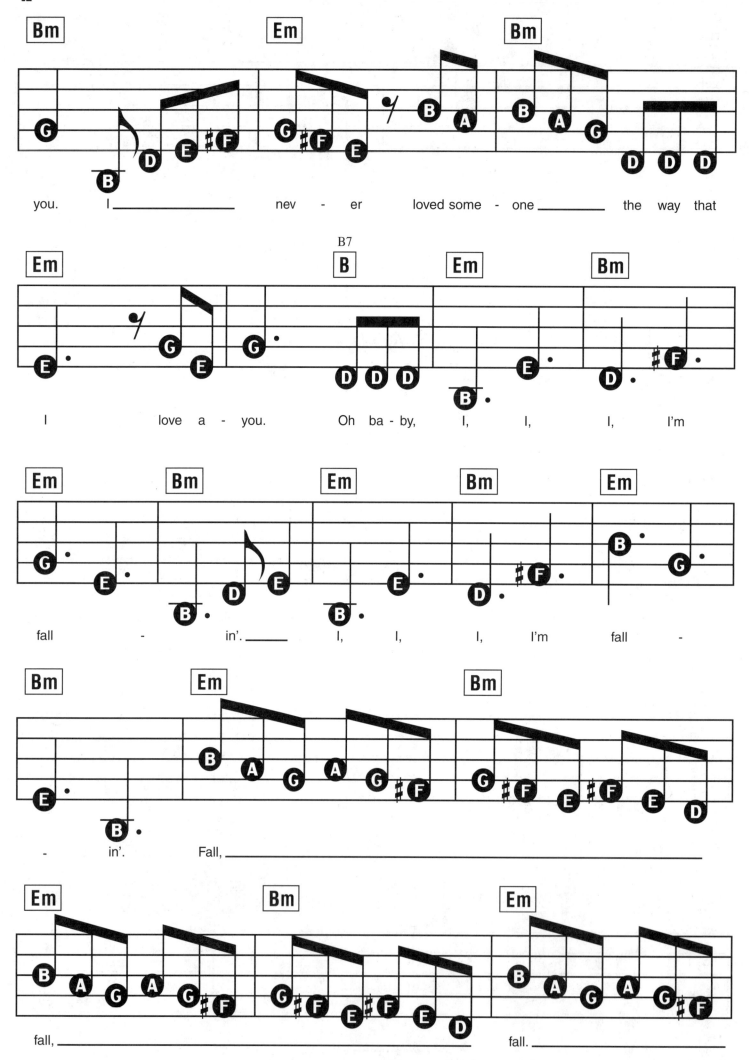

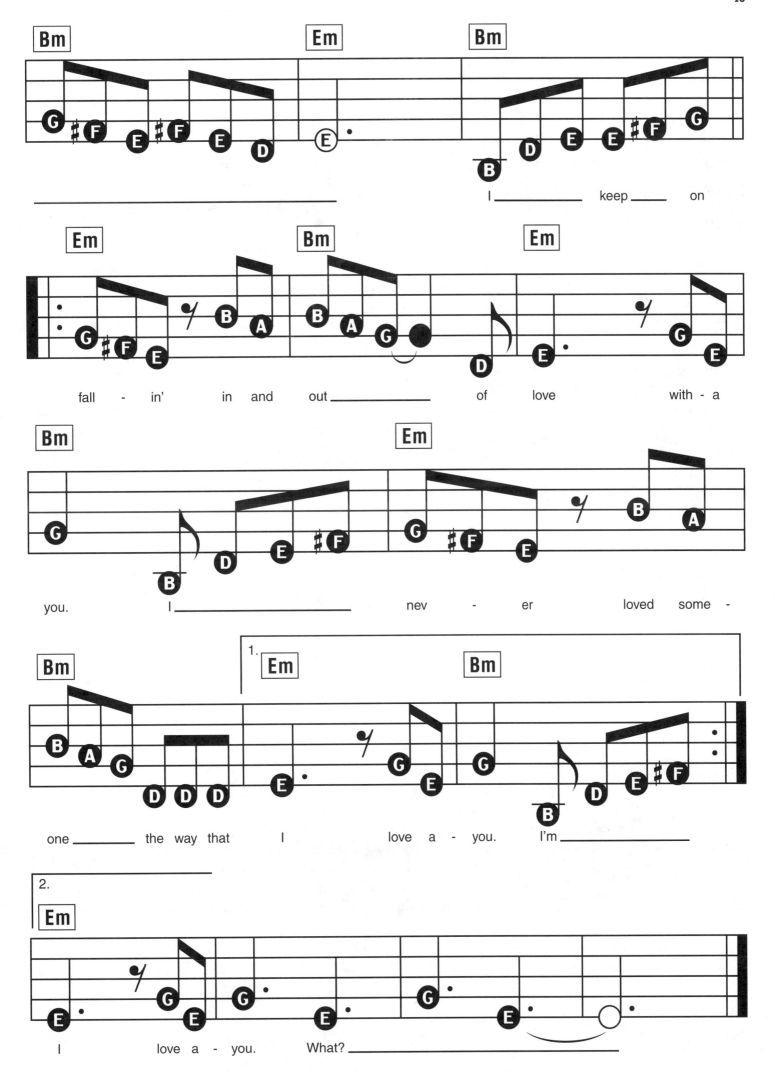

Hero

Registration 5
Rhythm: Rock or 8-Beat

Words and Music by Mariah Carey
and Walter Afanasieff

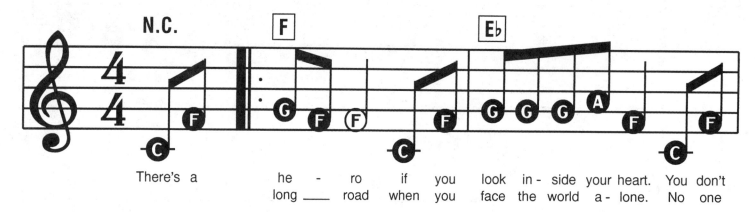

There's a / he - ro if you look in - side your heart. You don't
long ___ road when you face the world a - lone. No one

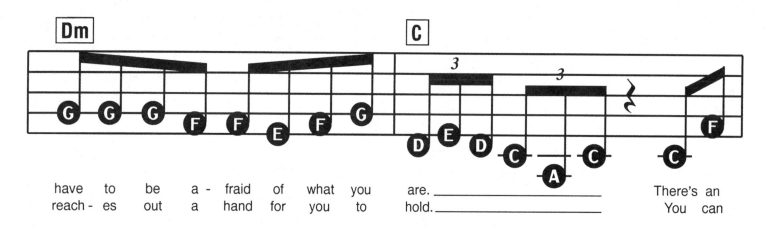

have to be a - fraid of what you are. ___ There's an
reach - es out a hand for you to hold. ___ You can

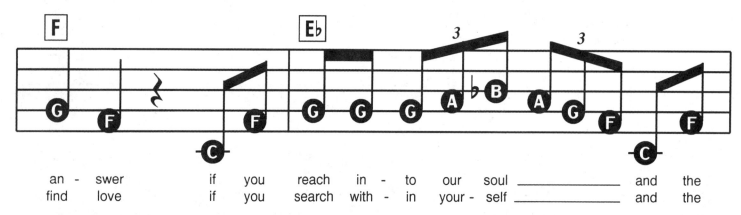

an - swer if you reach in - to our soul ___ and the
find love if you search with - in your - self ___ and the

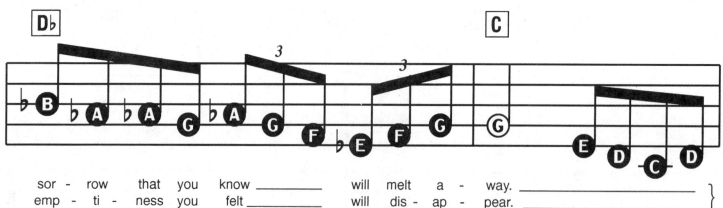

sor - row that you know ___ will melt a - way. ___
emp - ti - ness you felt ___ will dis - ap - pear. ___

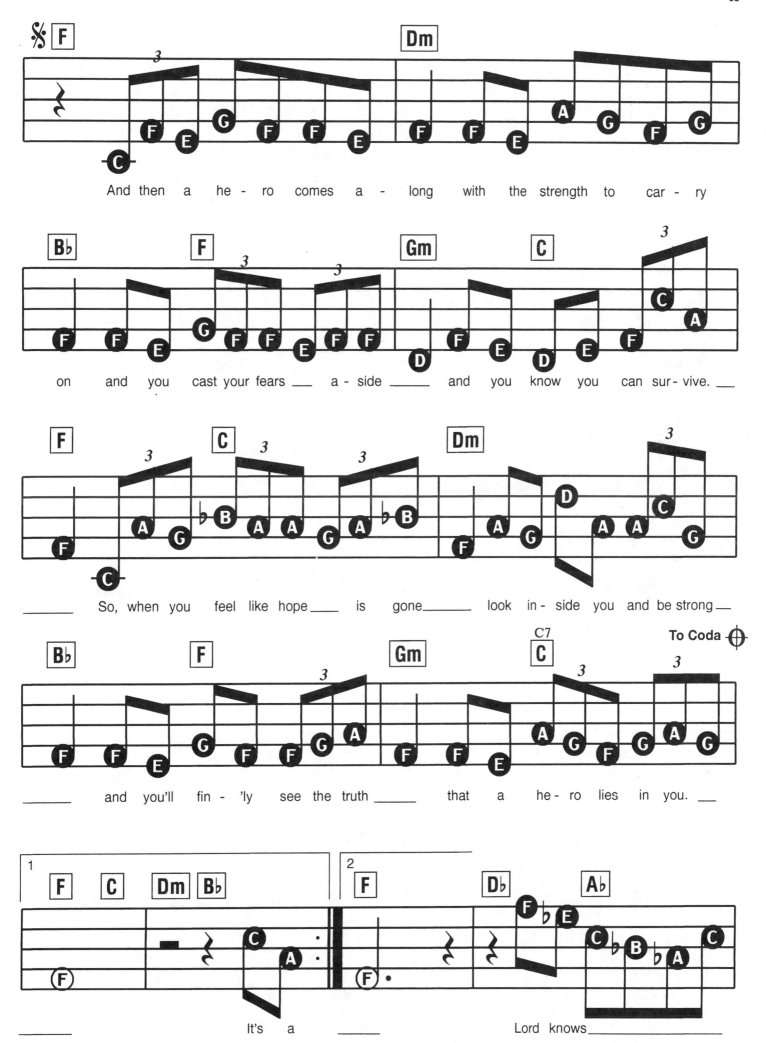

I Believe I Can Fly
from SPACE JAM

Registration 3
Rhythm: Pop or Rock

Words and Music by
Robert Kelly

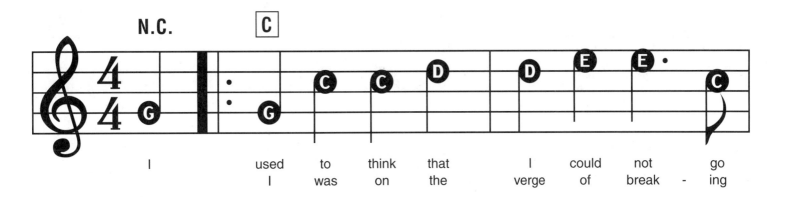

I used to think that I could not go
I was on that the verge of break - ing

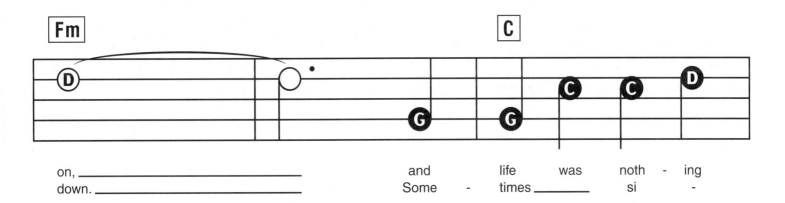

on, _____ and life was noth - ing
down. _____ Some - times _____ si -

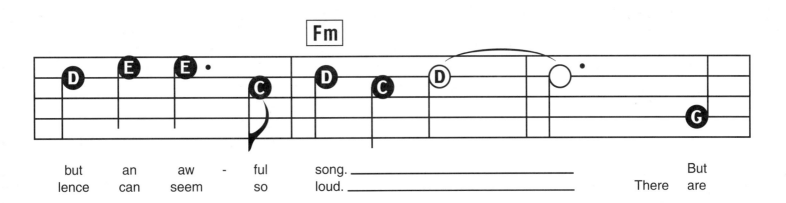

but an aw - ful song. _____ But
lence can seem so loud. _____ There are

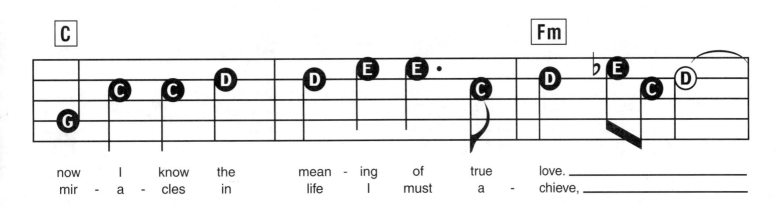

now I know the mean - ing of true love. _____
mir - a - cles in life I must a - chieve, _____

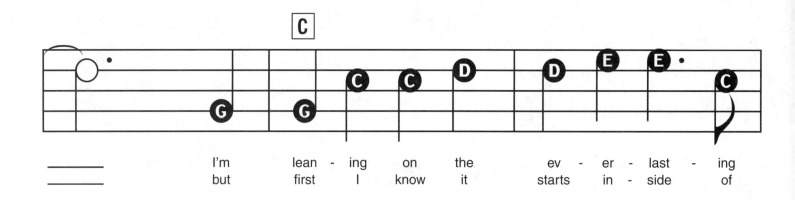

I'm lean - ing on the ev - er - last - ing
but first I know it starts in - side of

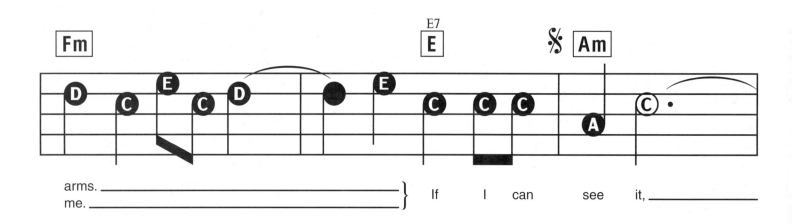

arms. _____
me. _____ } If I can see it, _____

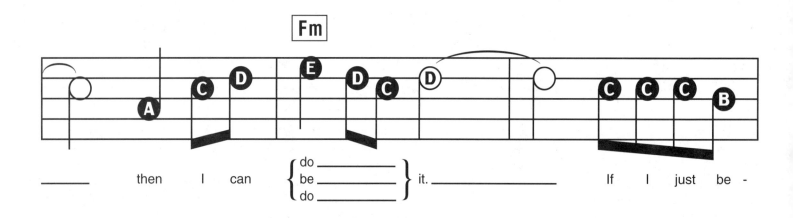

_____ then I can { do _____ / be _____ / do _____ } it. _____ If I just be -

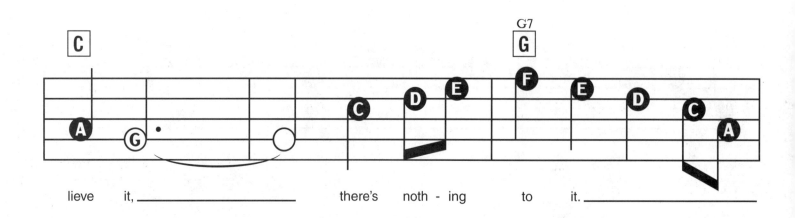

lieve it, _____ there's noth - ing to it. _____

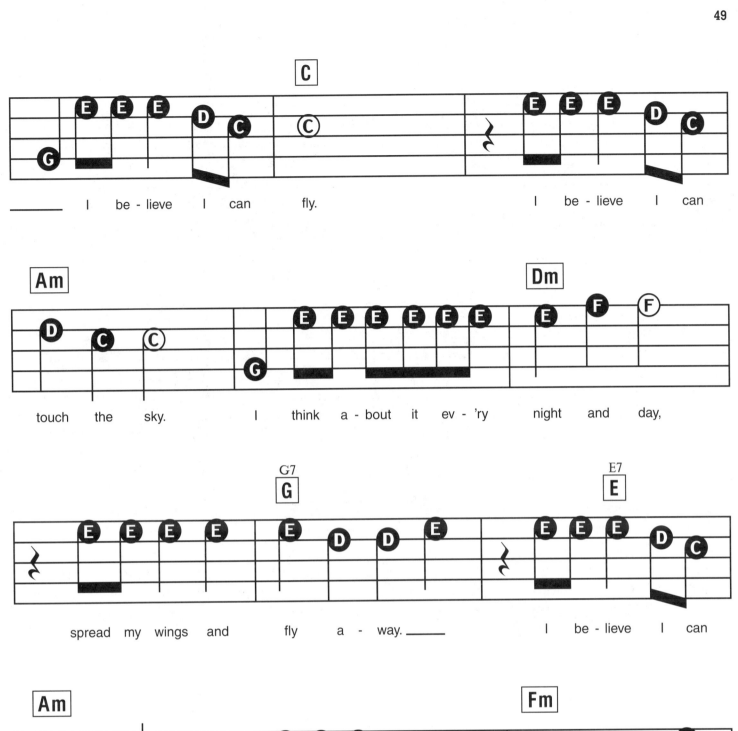

____ I be - lieve I can fly. I be - lieve I can

touch the sky. I think a - bout it ev - 'ry night and day,

spread my wings and fly a - way. ____ I be - lieve I can

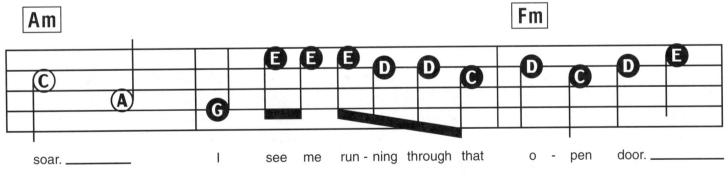

soar. ____ I see me run - ning through that o - pen door. ____

To Coda ⊕

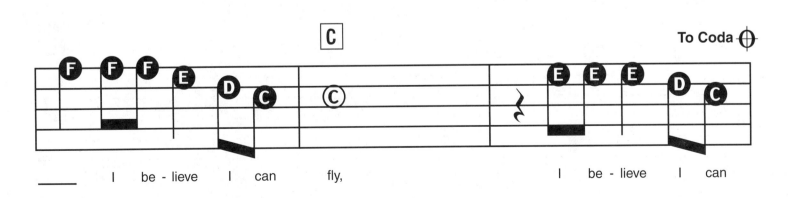

____ I be - lieve I can fly, I be - lieve I can

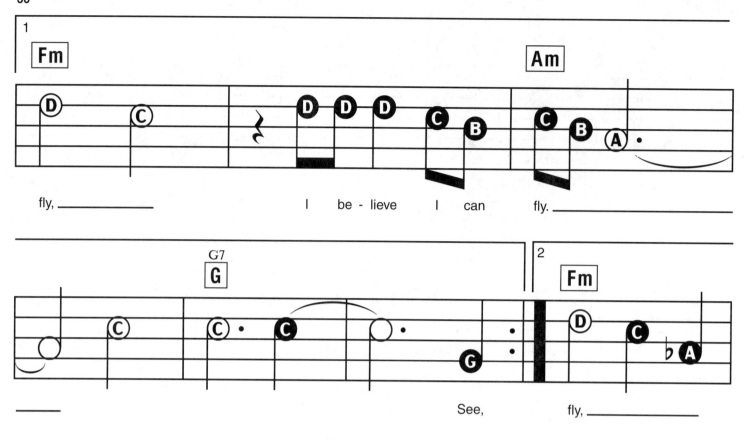

fly, _____ I be-lieve I can fly. _____

_____ See, fly, _____

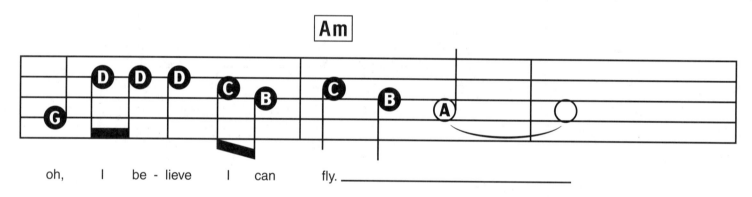

oh, I be-lieve I can fly. _____

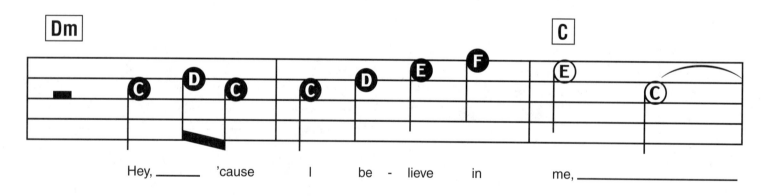

Hey, _____ 'cause I be-lieve in me, _____

D.S. al Coda
(Return to ⅜
Play to ⊕ and
Skip to Coda)

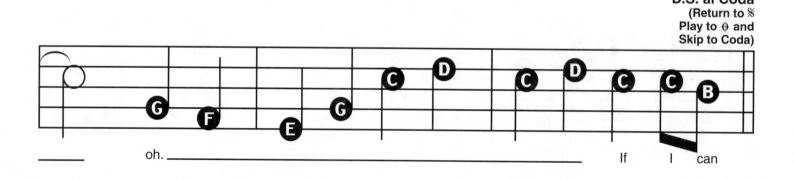

_____ oh. _____ If I can

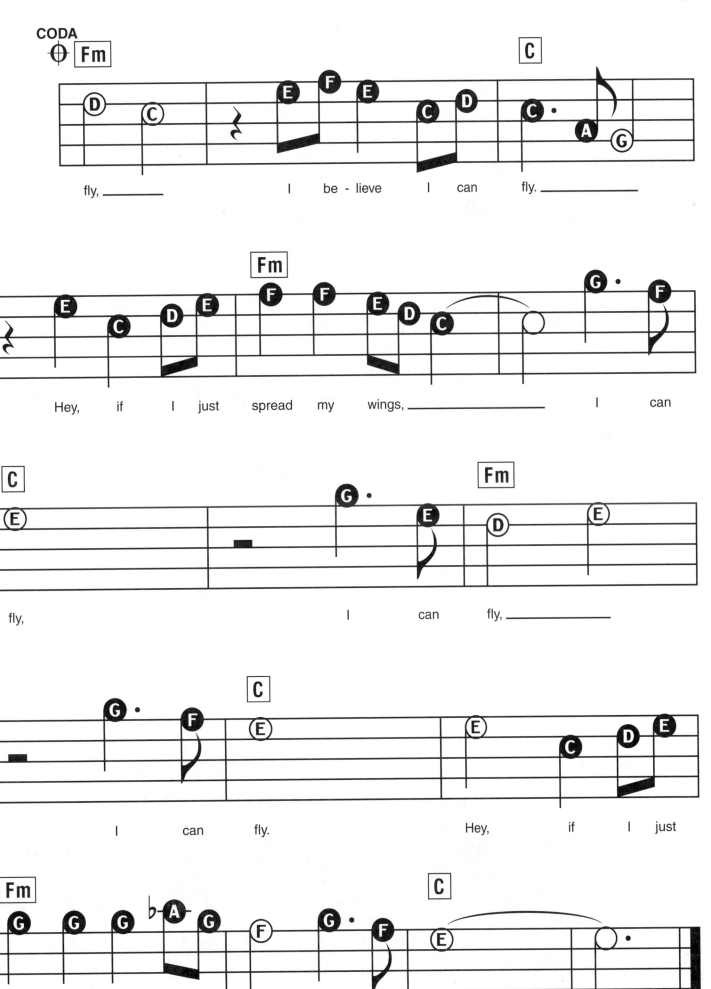

Home

Registration 8
Rhythm: 4/4 Ballad or 8-Beat

Words and Music by Amy Foster-Gillies,
Michael Bublé and Alan Chang

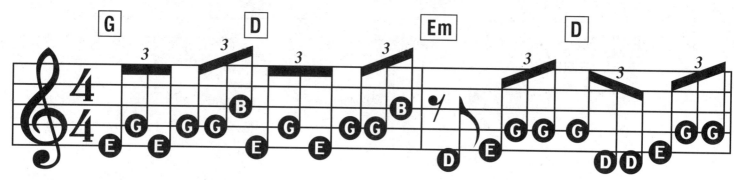

An - oth - er sum - mer day has come and gone a - way in Par - is and Rome, but I wan - na go

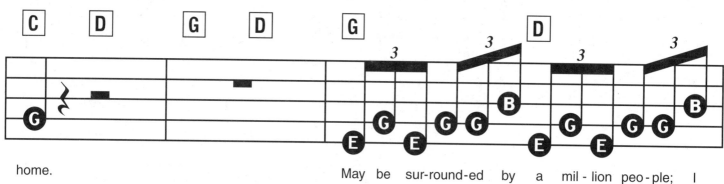

home. May be sur - round - ed by a mil - lion peo - ple; I

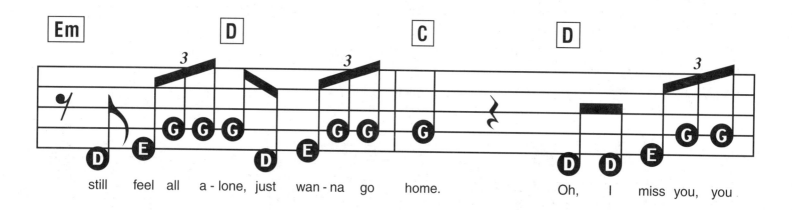

still feel all a - lone, just wan - na go home. Oh, I miss you, you

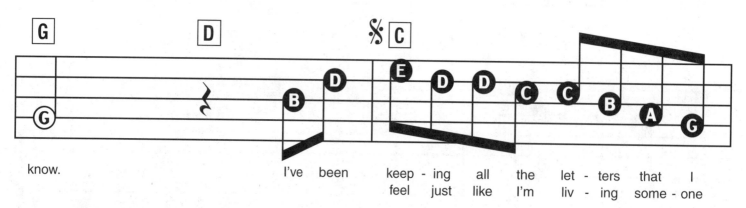

know. I've been keep - ing all the let - ters that I
feel just like I'm liv - ing some - one

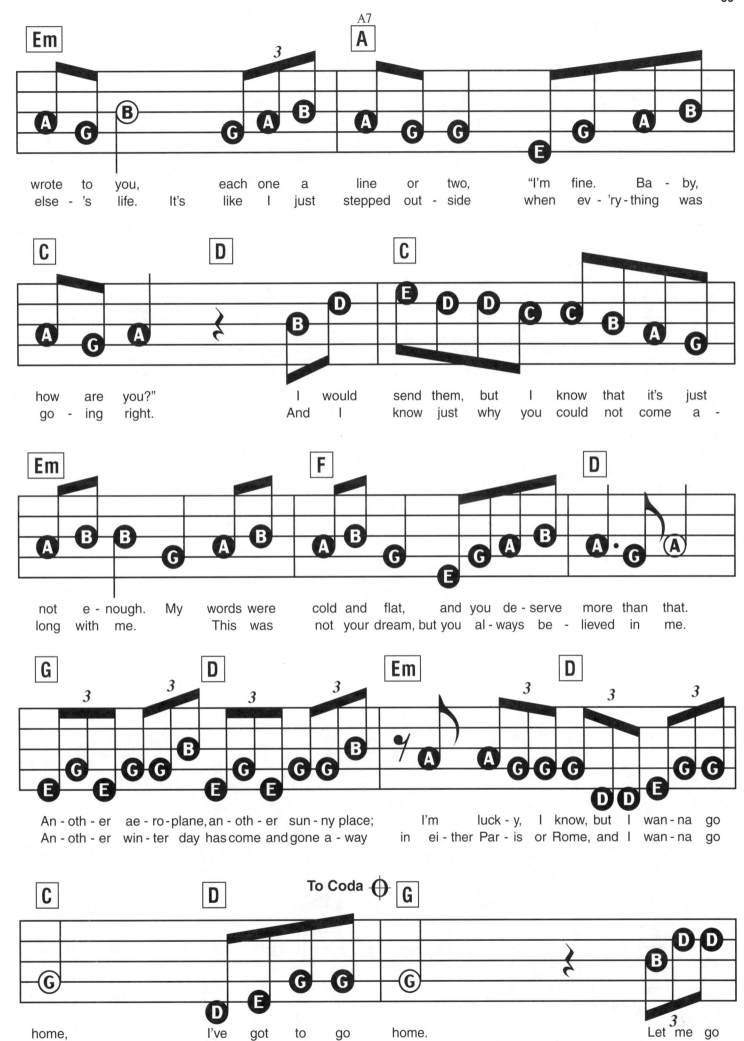

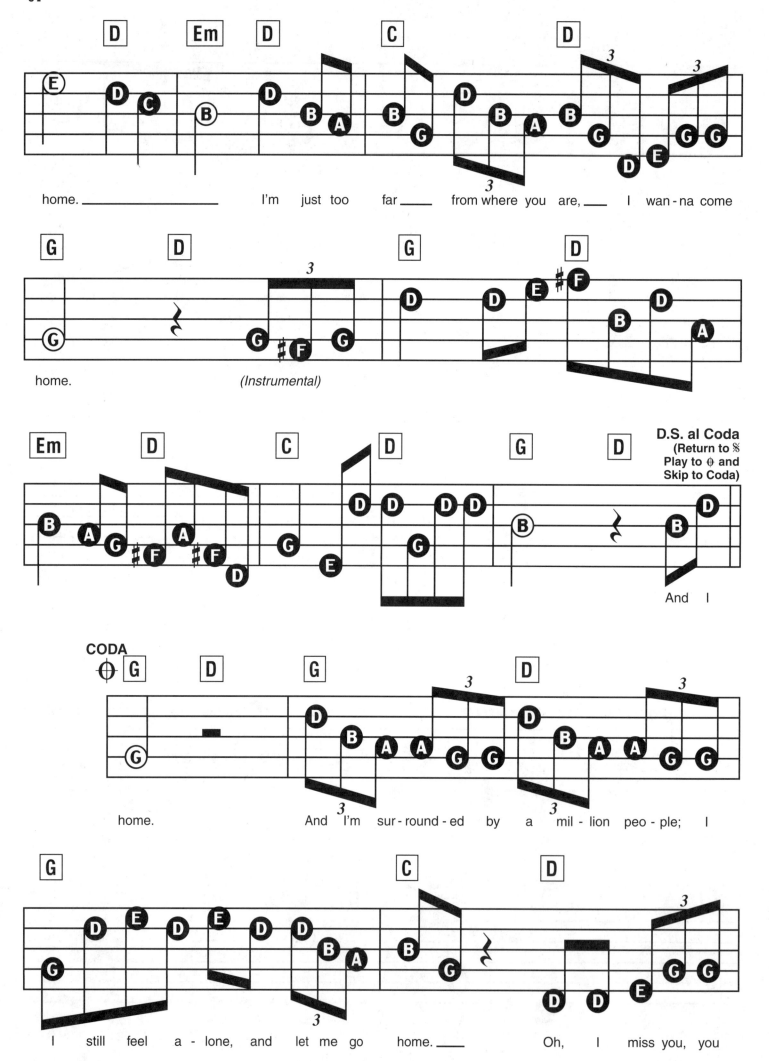

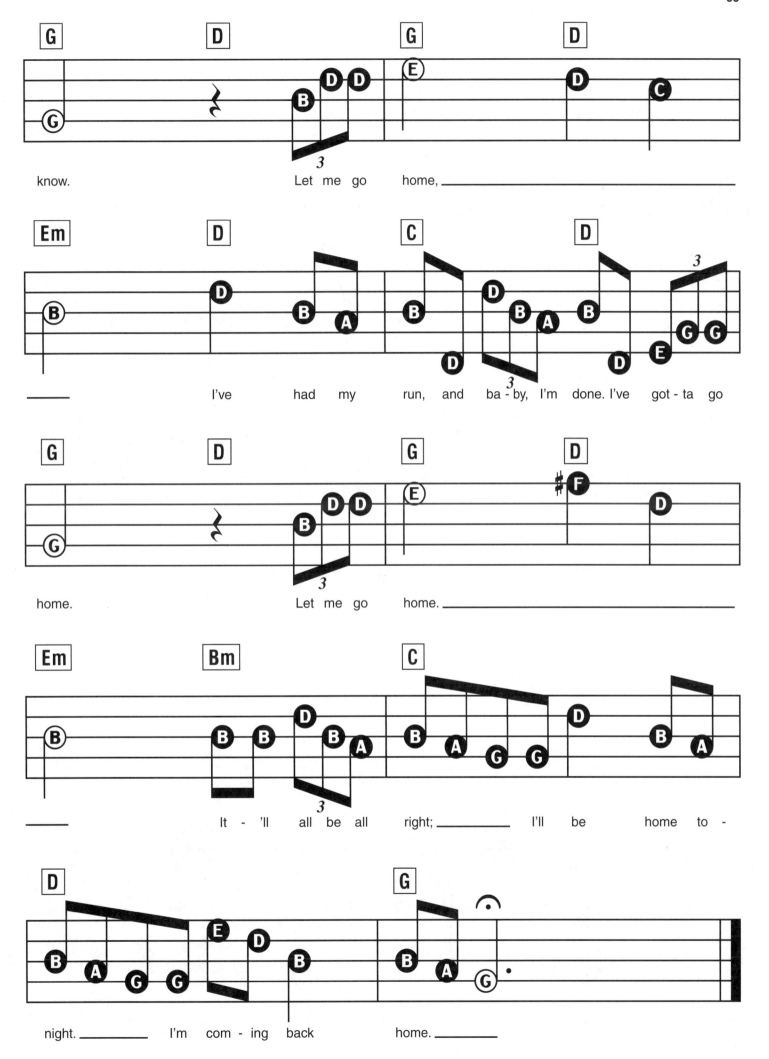

I Hope You Dance

Registration 8
Rhythm: Country Pop or Ballad

Words and Music by Tia Sillers
and Mark D. Sanders

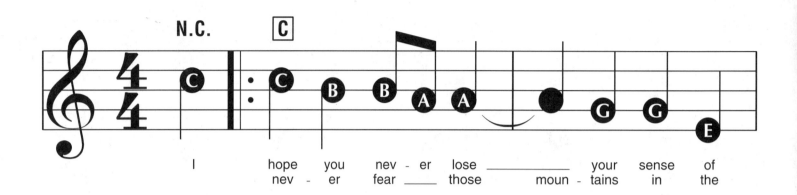

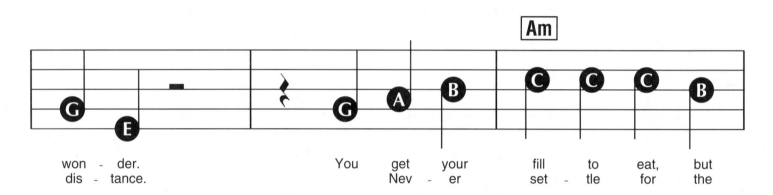

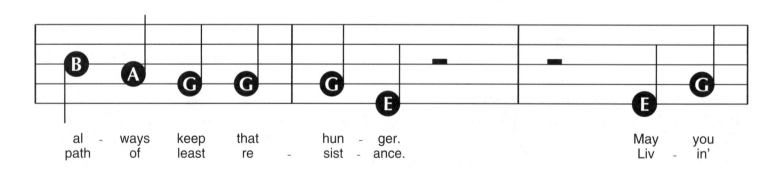

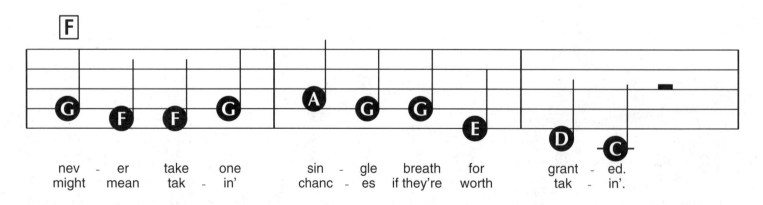

57

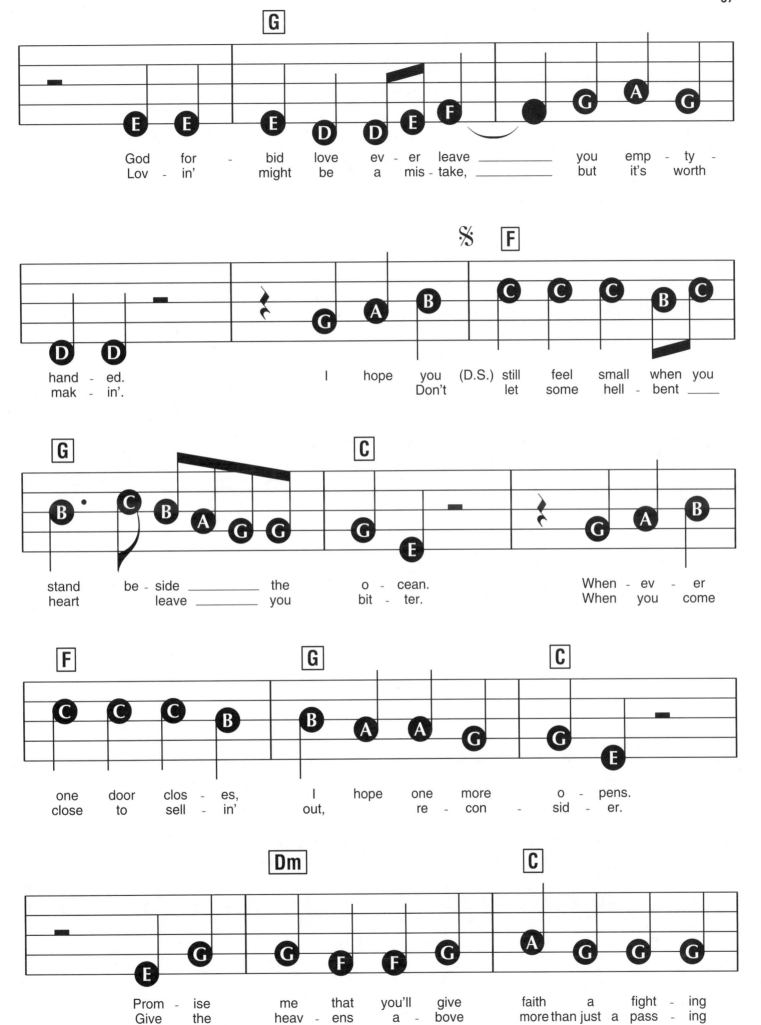

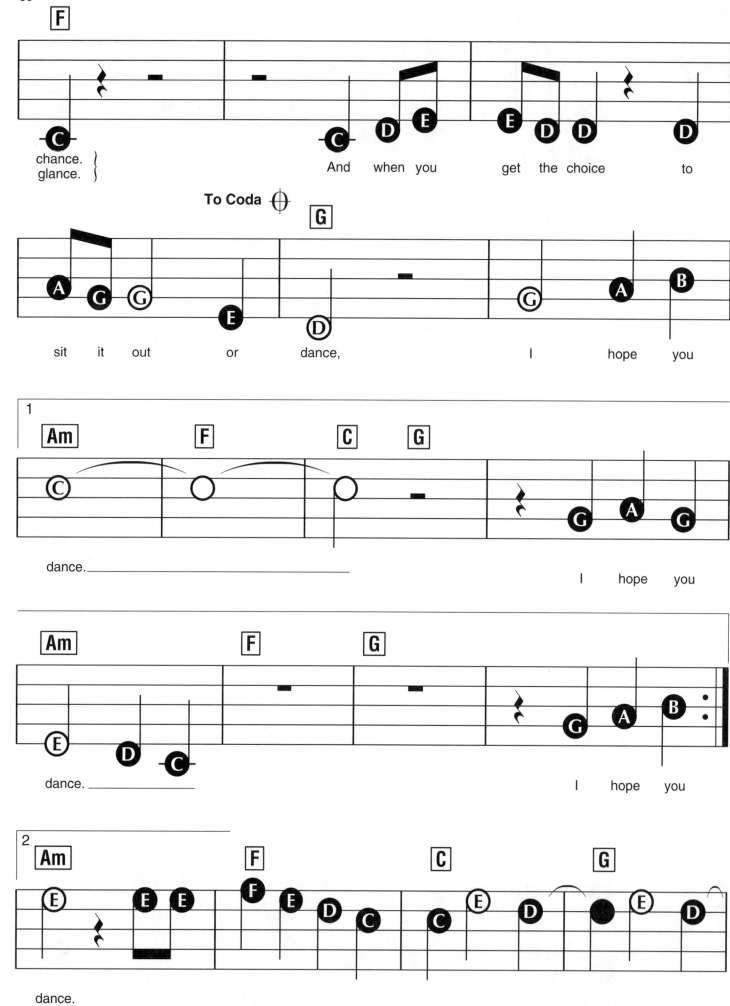

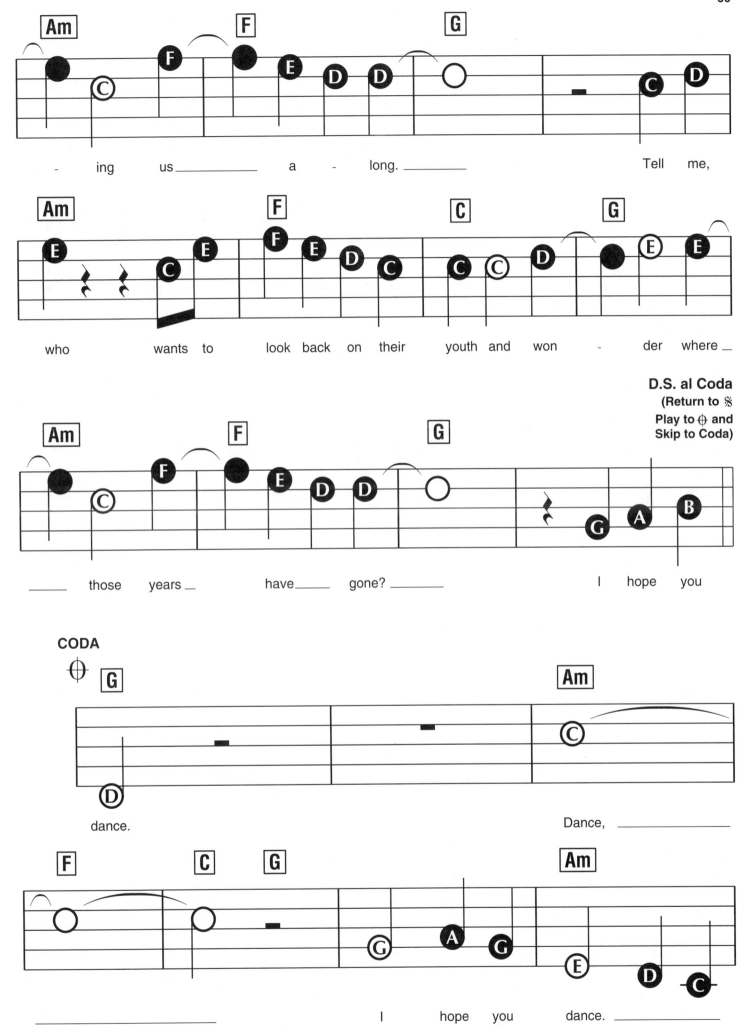

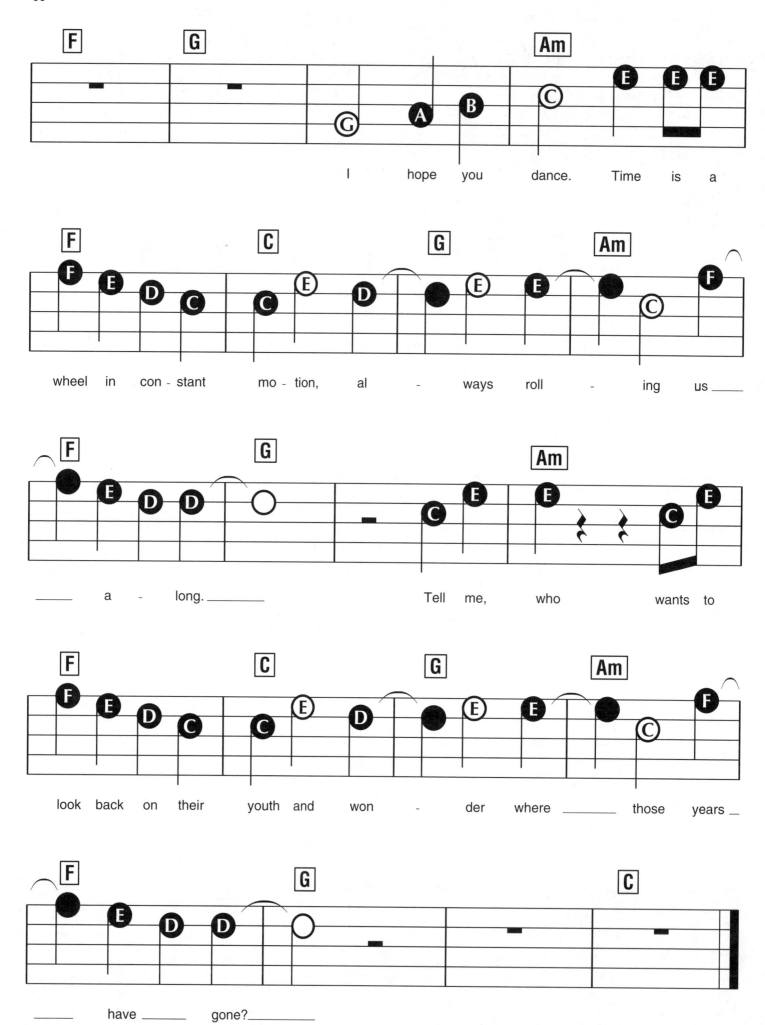

I'll Be

Registration 4
Rhythm: Waltz

Words and Music by
Edwin McCain

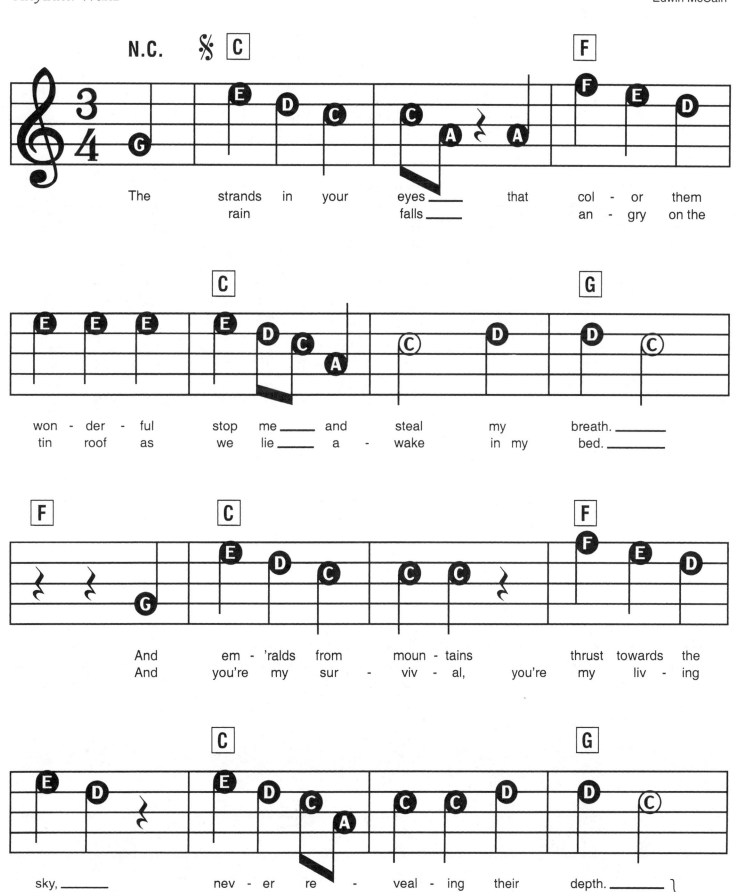

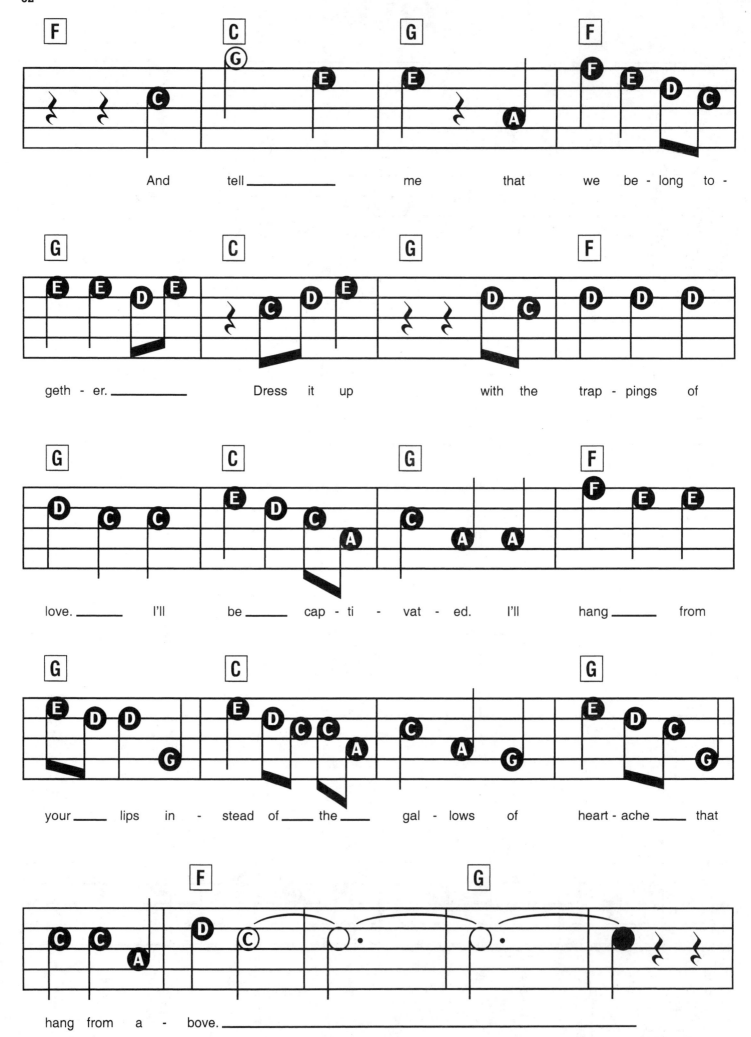

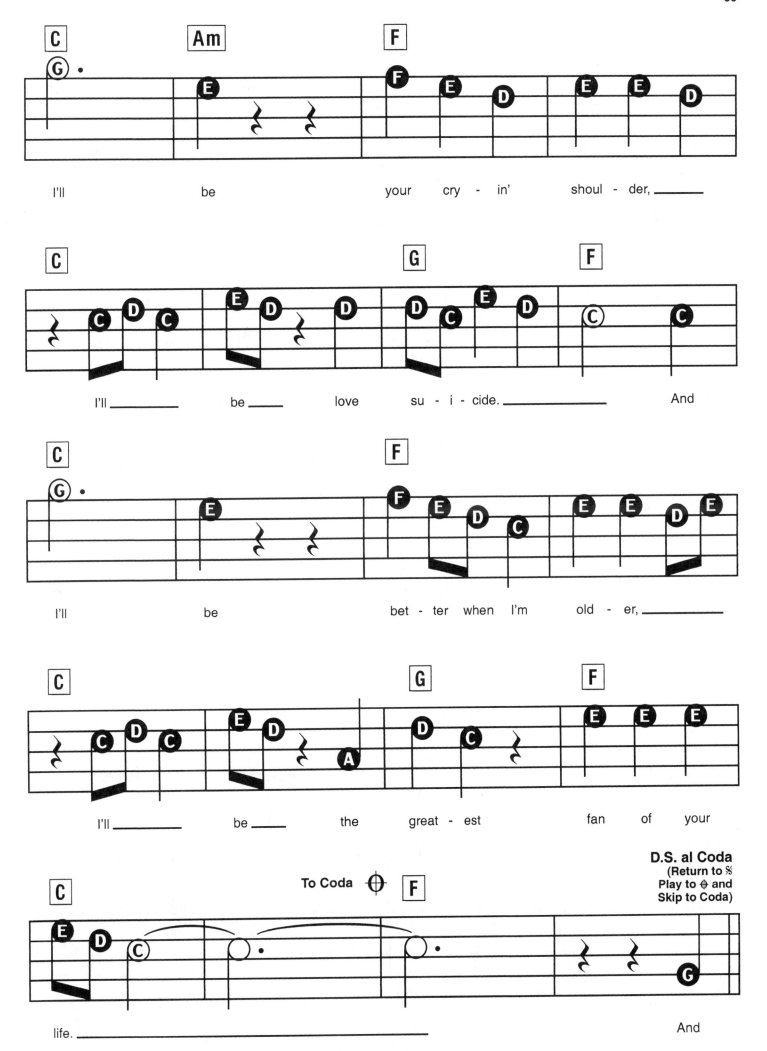

CODA

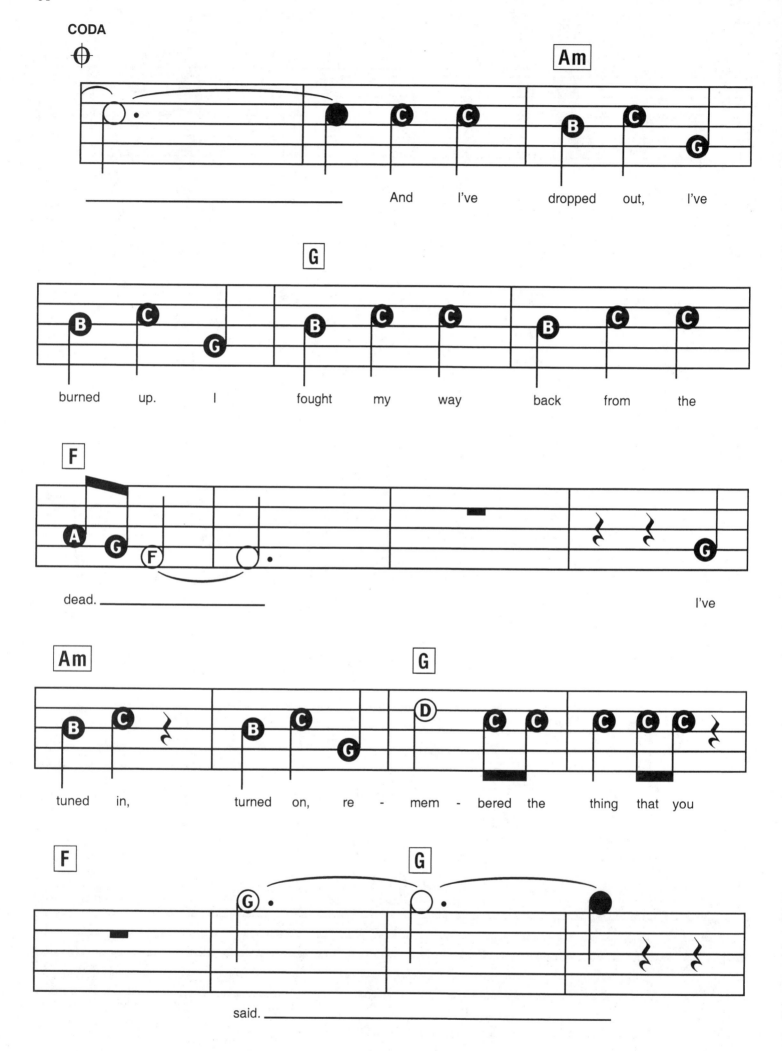

Am

And I've dropped out, I've

G

burned up. I fought my way back from the

F

dead. I've

Am   **G**

tuned in, turned on, re - mem - bered the thing that you

F   **G**

said.

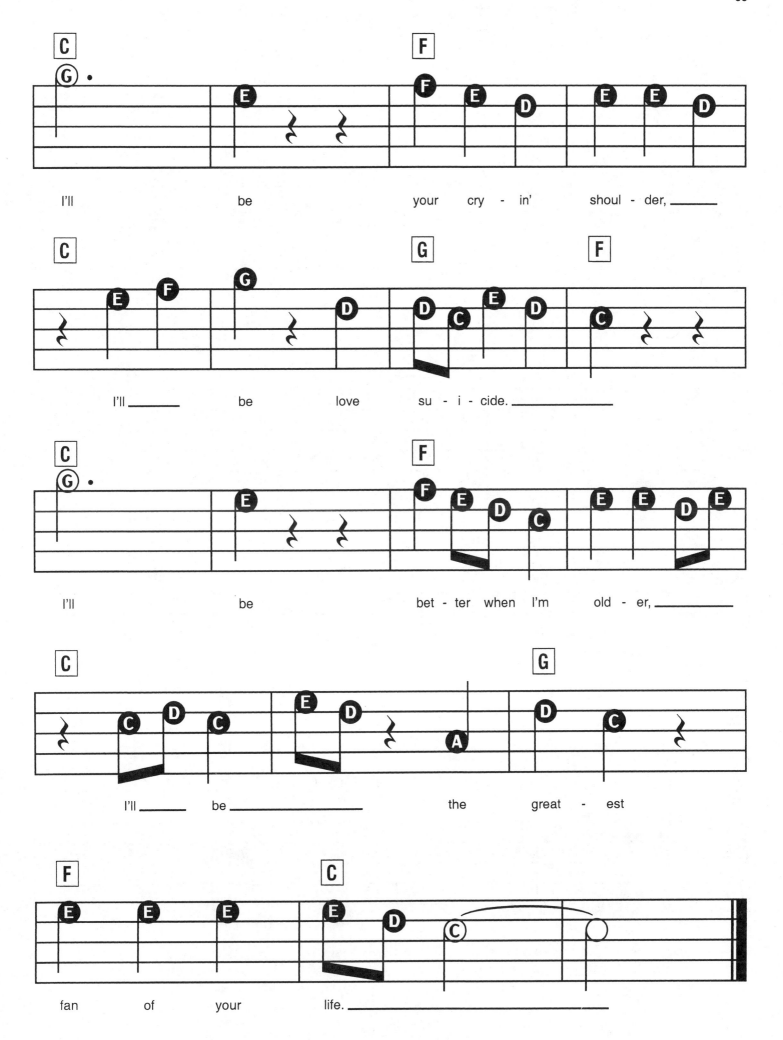

I Will Remember You
Theme from THE BROTHERS McMULLEN

Registration 1
Rhythm: Ballad

Words and Music by Sarah McLachlan,
Seamus Egan and Dave Merenda

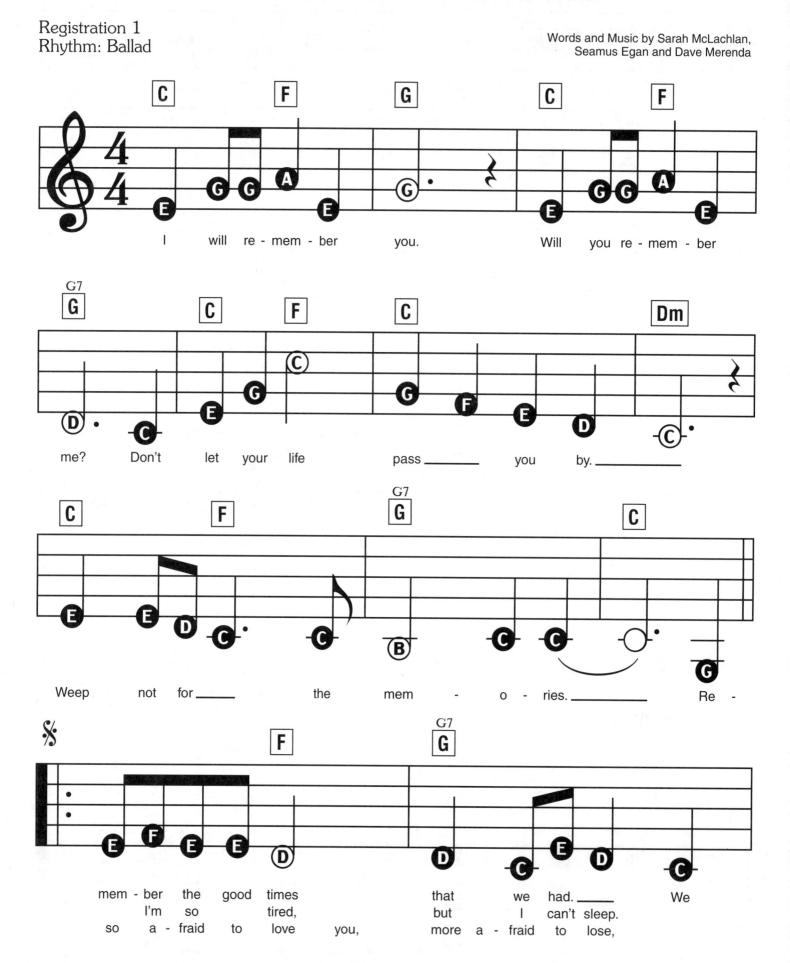

67

68

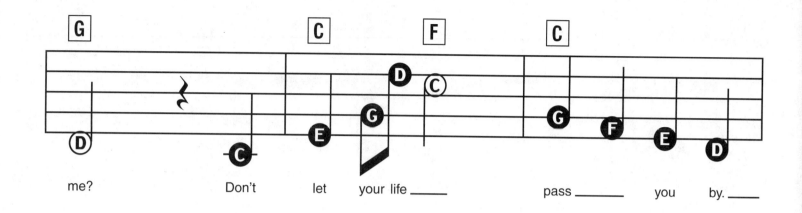

me?   Don't   let   your life _____   pass _____ you   by. _____

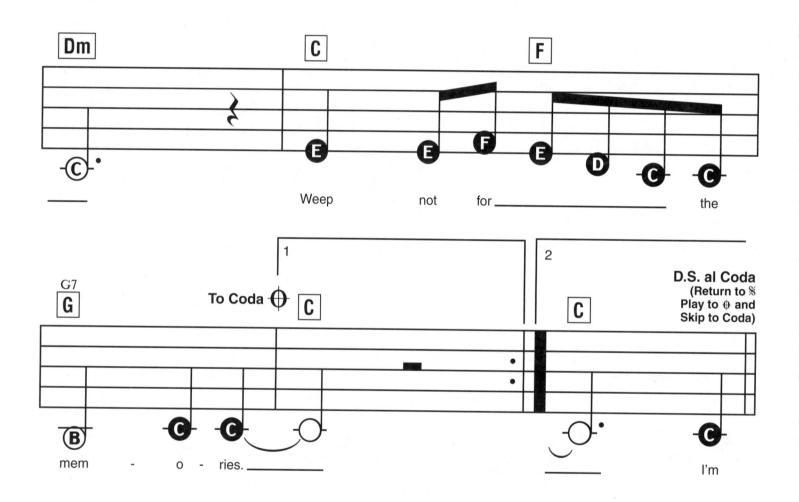

_____   Weep   not   for _____ the

D.S. al Coda
(Return to ⅗
Play to ⊕ and
Skip to Coda)

To Coda ⊕

mem - o - ries. _____   _____   I'm

CODA ⊕

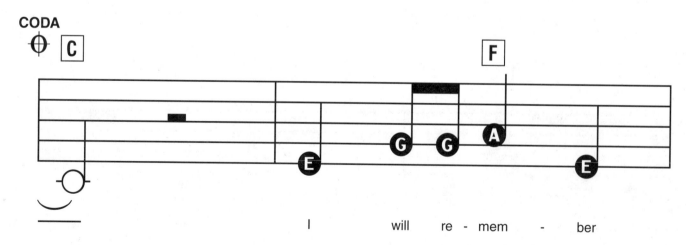

_____   I   will   re - mem - ber

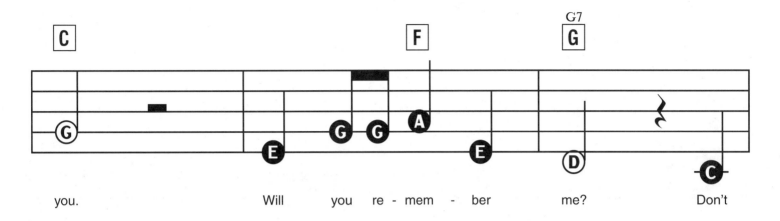

you. Will you re - mem - ber me? Don't

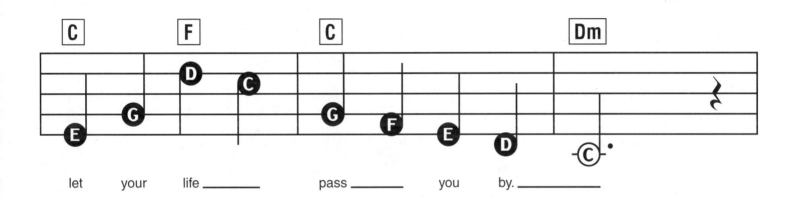

let your life _____ pass _____ you by. _____

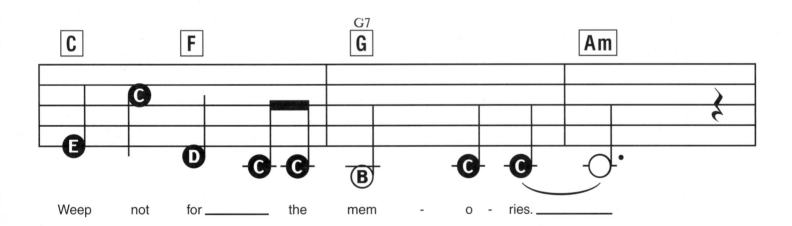

Weep not for _____ the mem - o - ries. _____

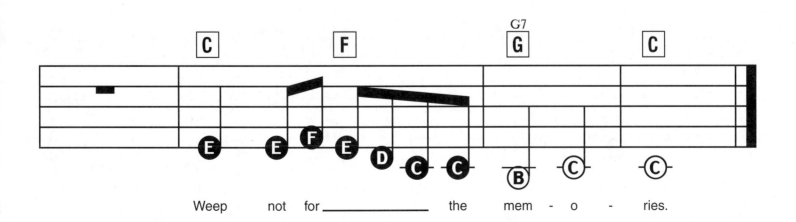

Weep not for _____ the mem - o - ries.

Landslide

Registration 4
Rhythm: Fox Trot or Ballad

Words and Music by
Stevie Nicks

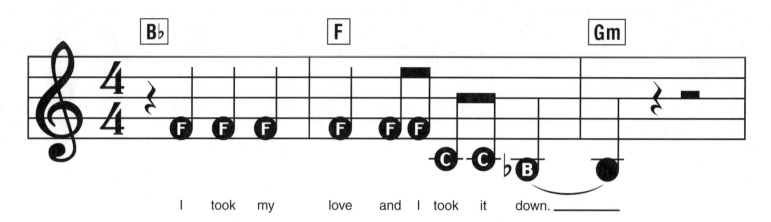

I took my love and I took it down.

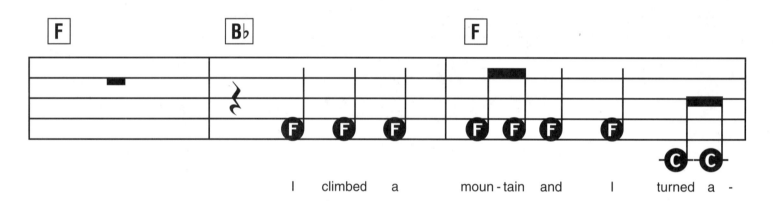

I climbed a moun-tain and I turned a-

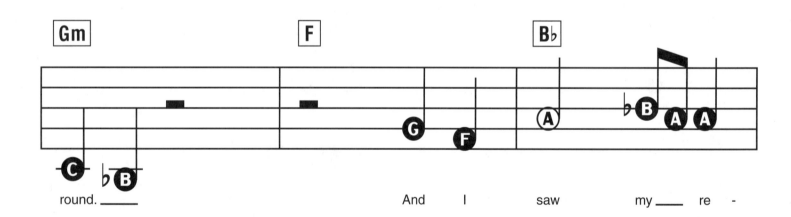

round. And I saw my ___ re-

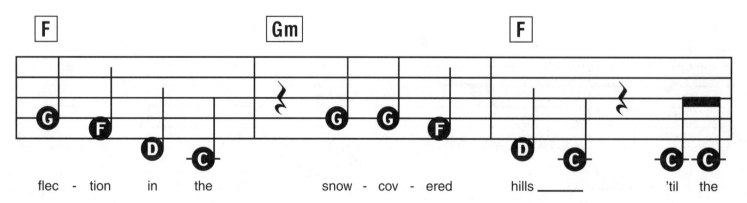

flec-tion in the snow-cov-ered hills ___ 'til the

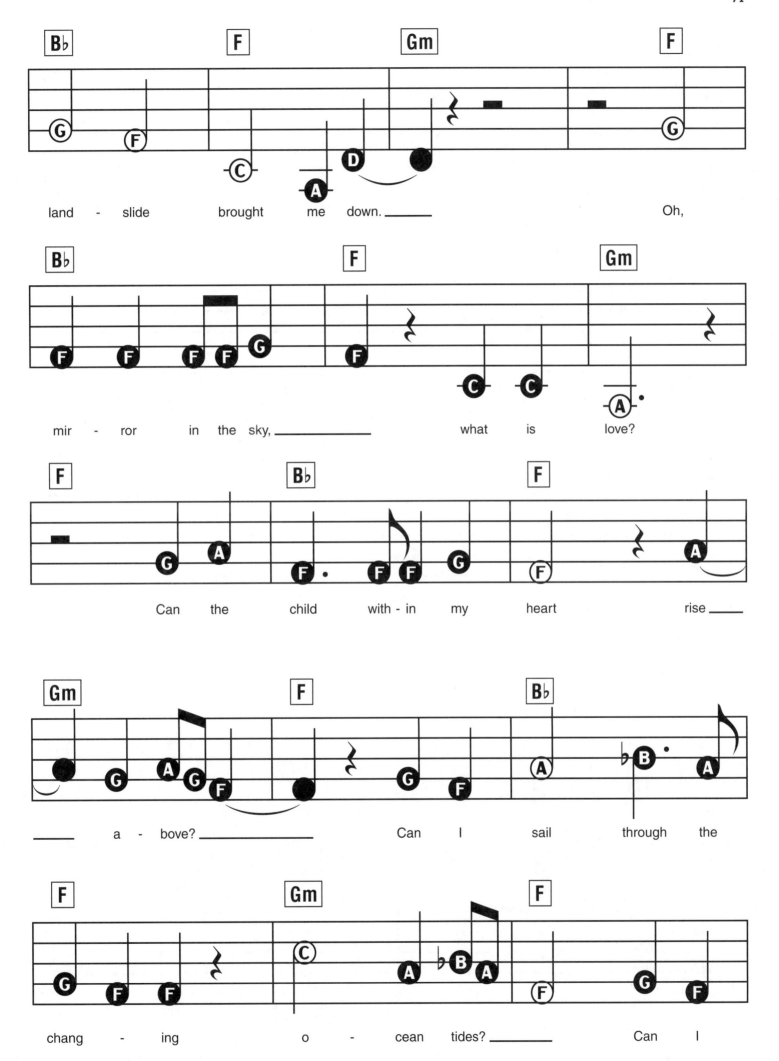

72

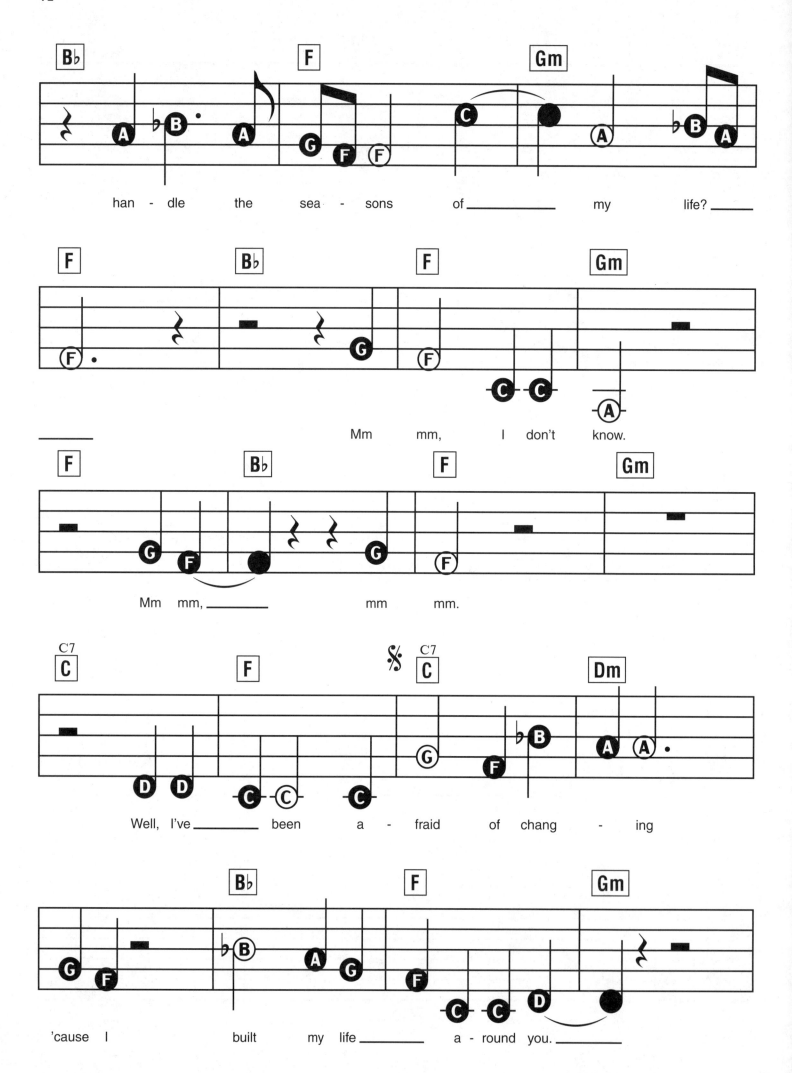

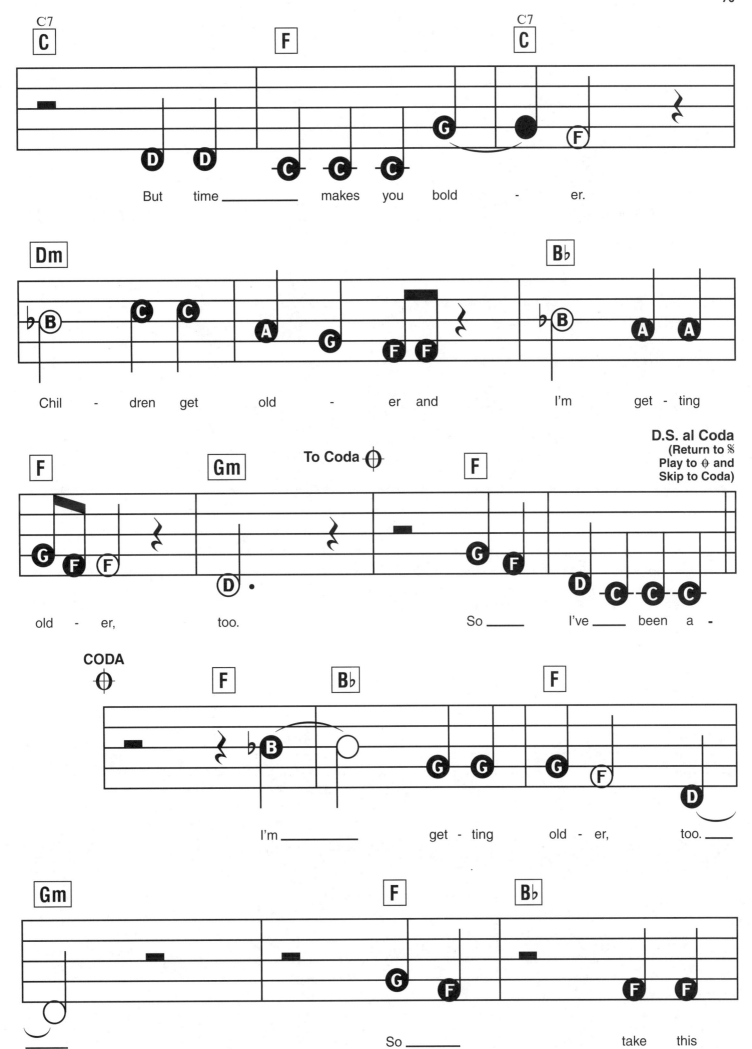

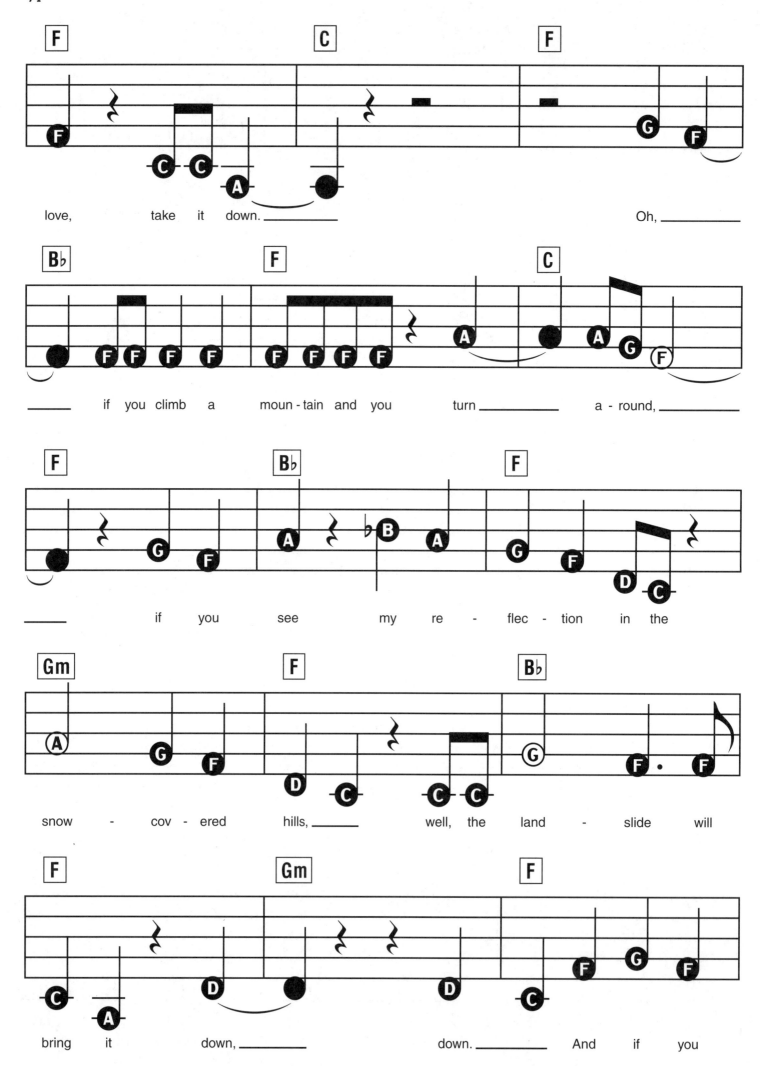

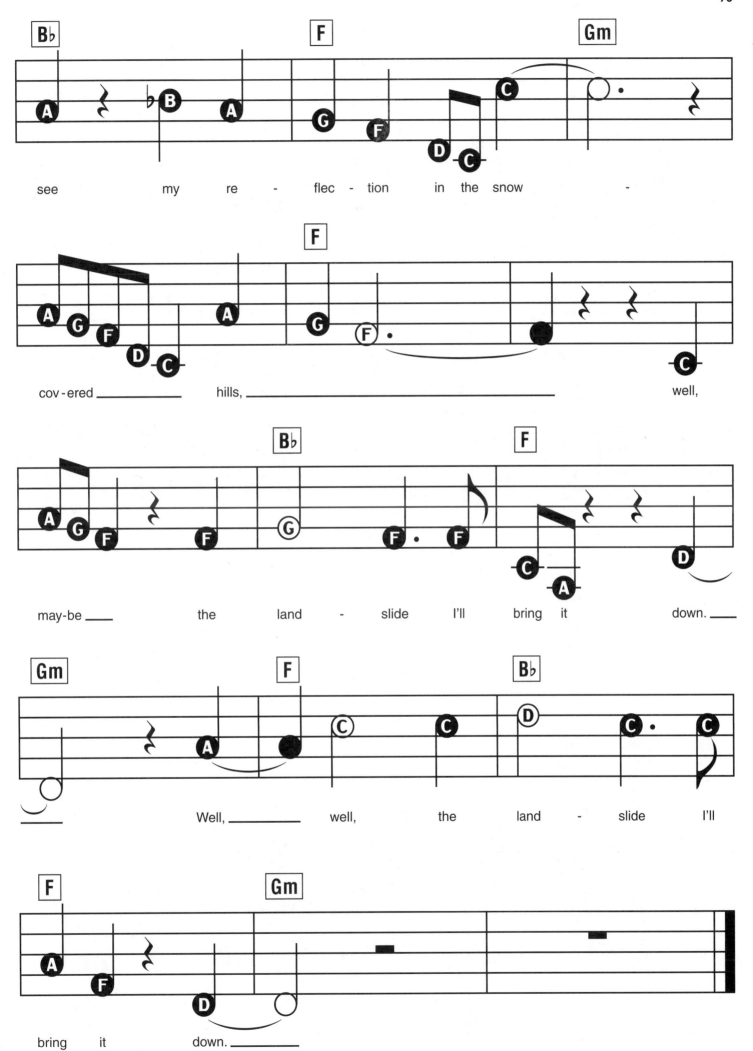

Listen to Your Heart

Registration 4
Rhythm: 8-Beat or Rock

Words and Music by Per Gessle
and Mats Persson

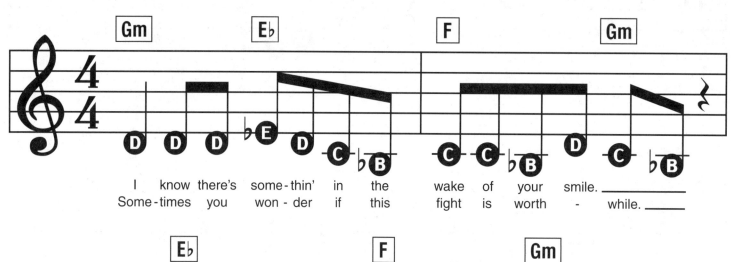

I know there's some-thin' in the wake of your smile. _____
Some-times you won-der if this fight is worth - while. _____

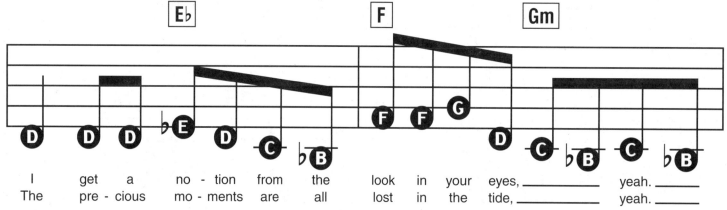

I get a no-tion from the look in your eyes, _____ yeah. _____
The pre-cious mo-ments are all lost in the tide, _____ yeah. _____

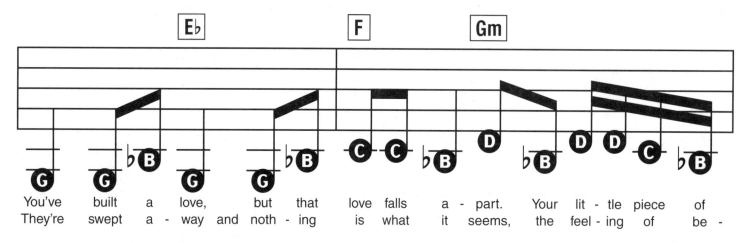

You've built a love, but that love falls a - part. Your lit-tle piece of
They're swept a - way and noth - ing is what it seems, the feel-ing of be -

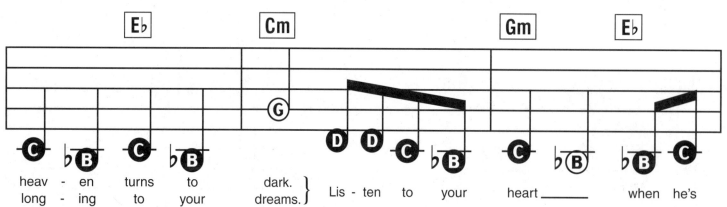

heav - en turns to dark. }
long - ing to your dreams. } Lis - ten to your heart _____ when he's

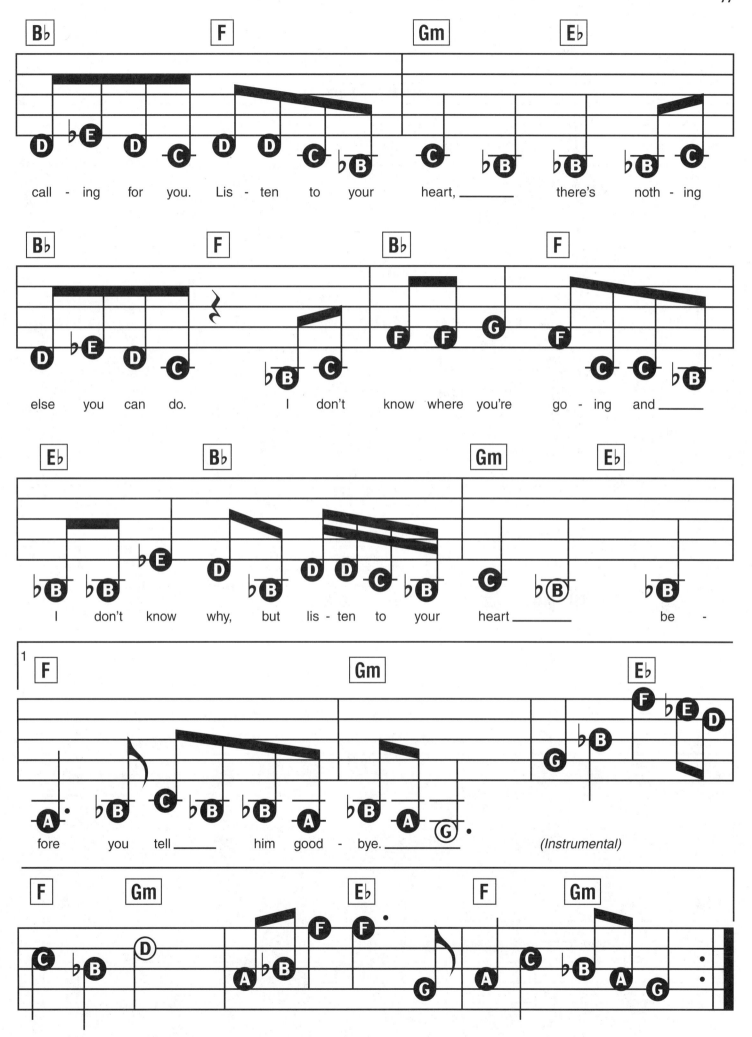

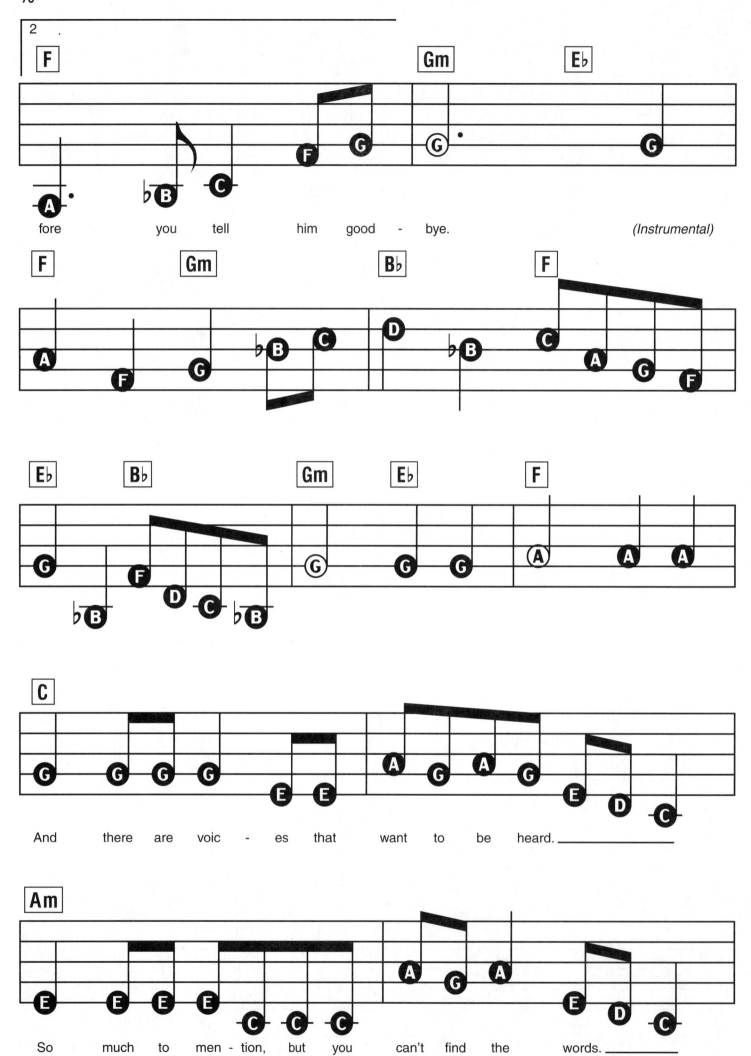

fore   you   tell   him   good - bye.   *(Instrumental)*

And   there   are   voic - es   that   want   to   be   heard. _____

So   much   to   men - tion,   but   you   can't   find   the   words. _____

100 Years

Registration 1
Rhythm: 8-Beat or Rock

Words and Music by
John Ondrasik

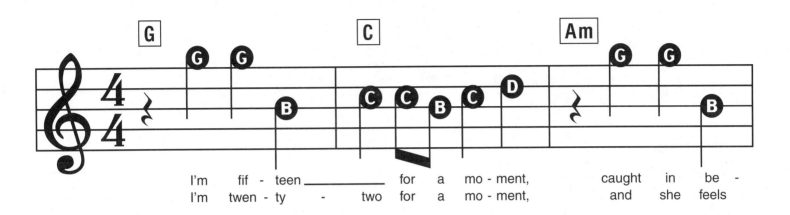

I'm fif - teen _____ for a mo - ment, caught in be -
I'm twen - ty - two for a mo - ment, and she feels

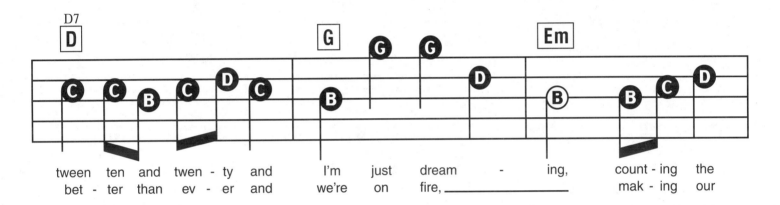

tween ten and twen - ty and I'm just dream - ing, count - ing the
bet - ter than ev - er and we're just on fire, _____ mak - ing our

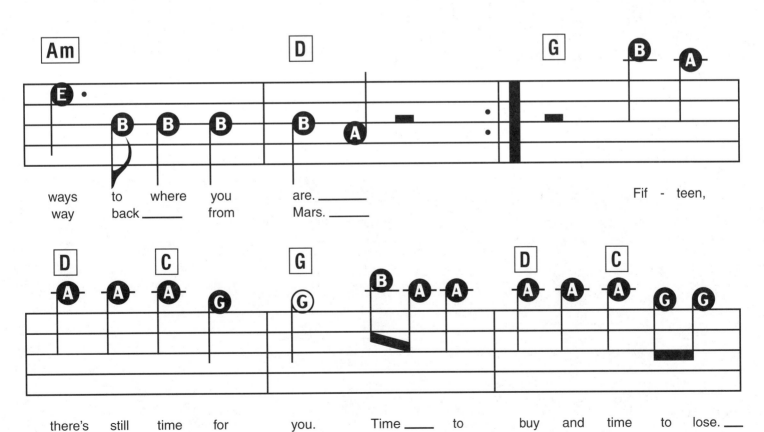

ways to where you are. _____ Fif - teen,
way back _____ you from Mars. _____

there's still time for you. Time _____ to buy and time to lose. _____

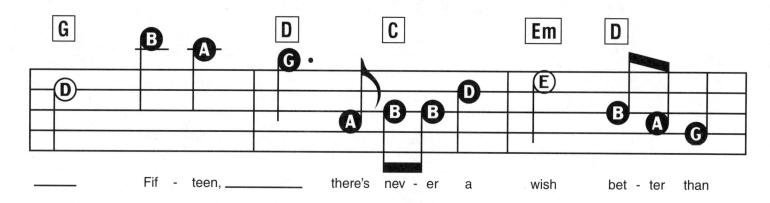

Fif - teen, _____ there's nev - er a wish bet - ter than

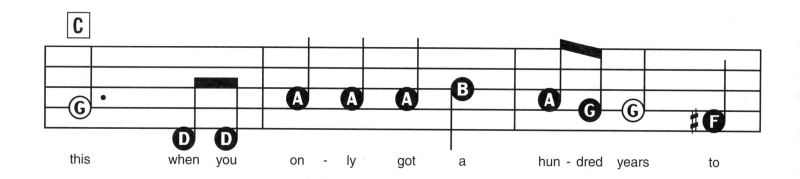

this when you on - ly got a hun - dred years to

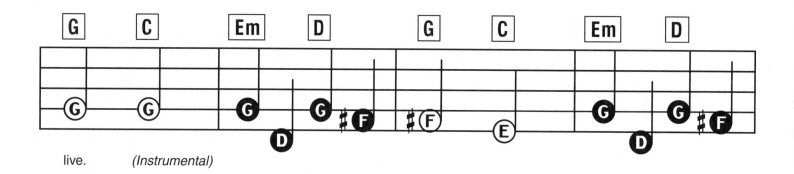

live. (Instrumental)

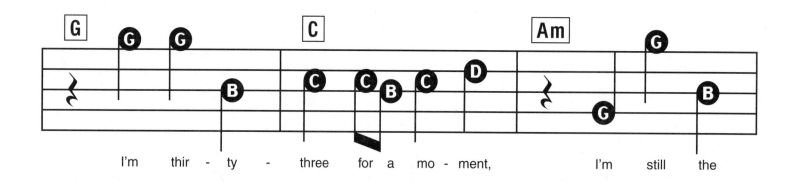

I'm thir - ty - three for a mo - ment, I'm still the

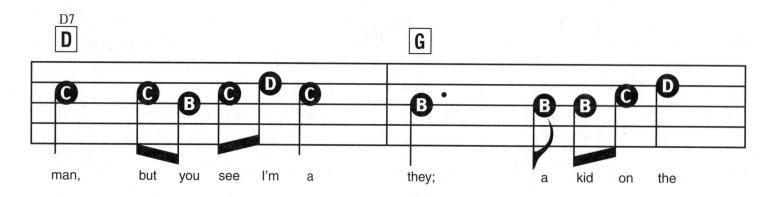

man, but you see I'm a they; a kid on the

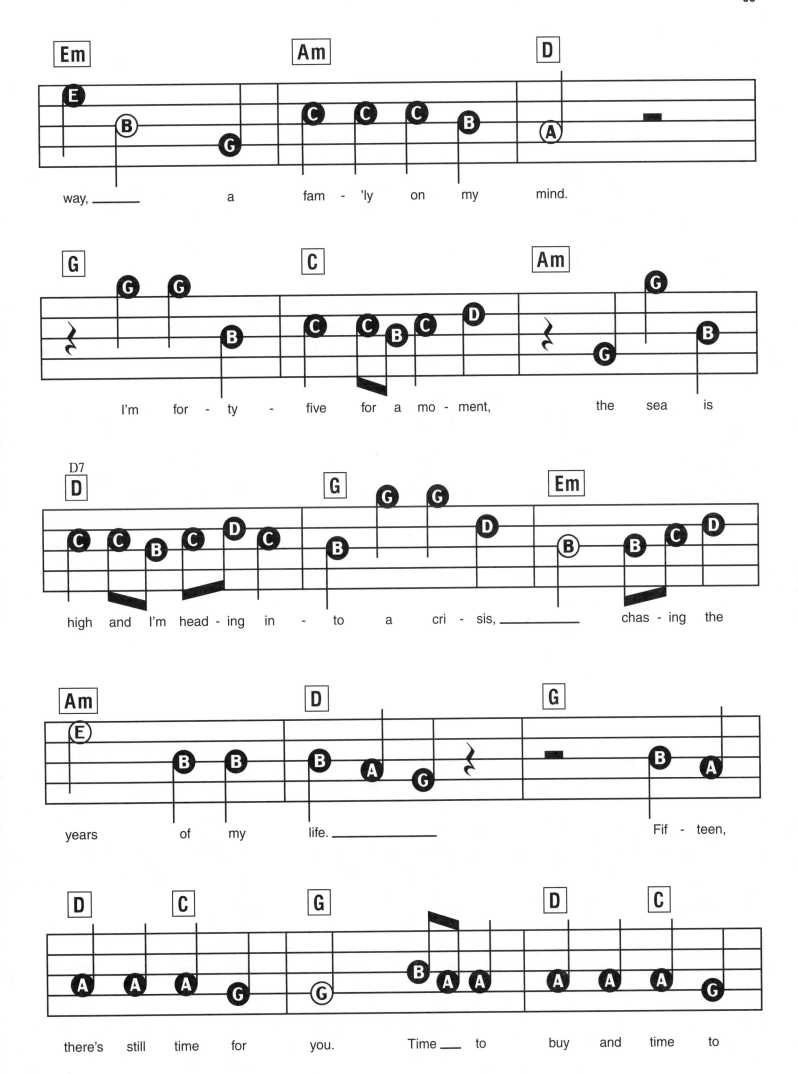

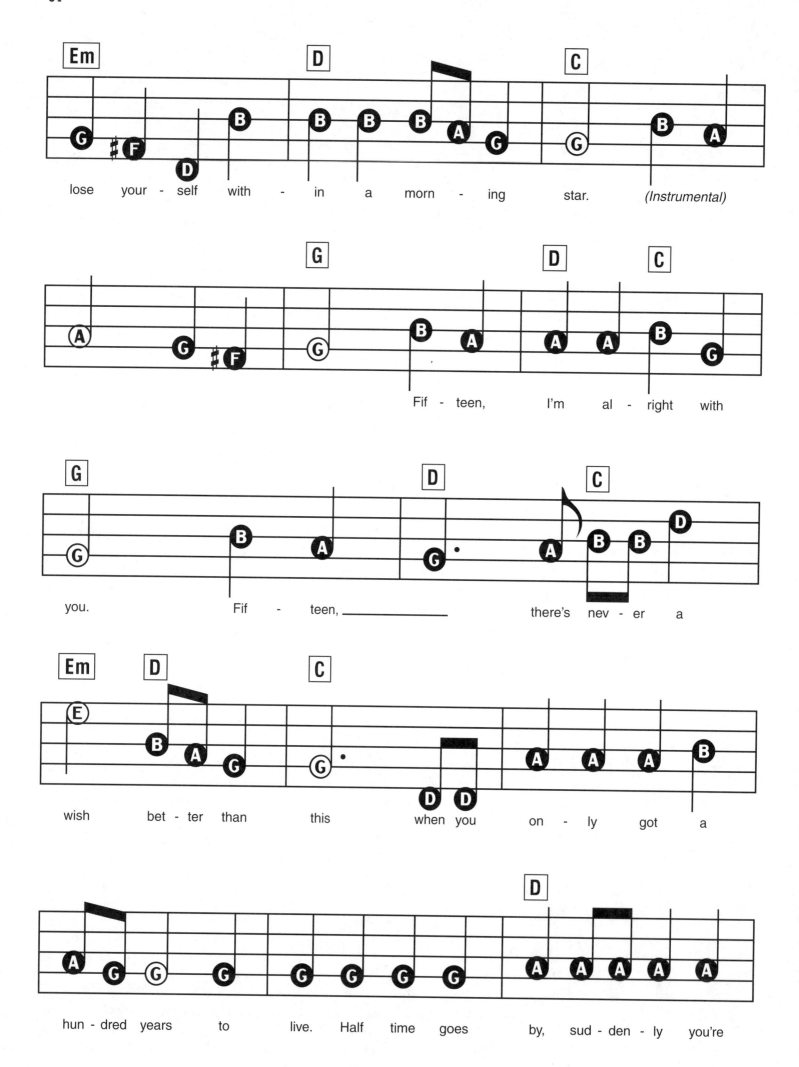

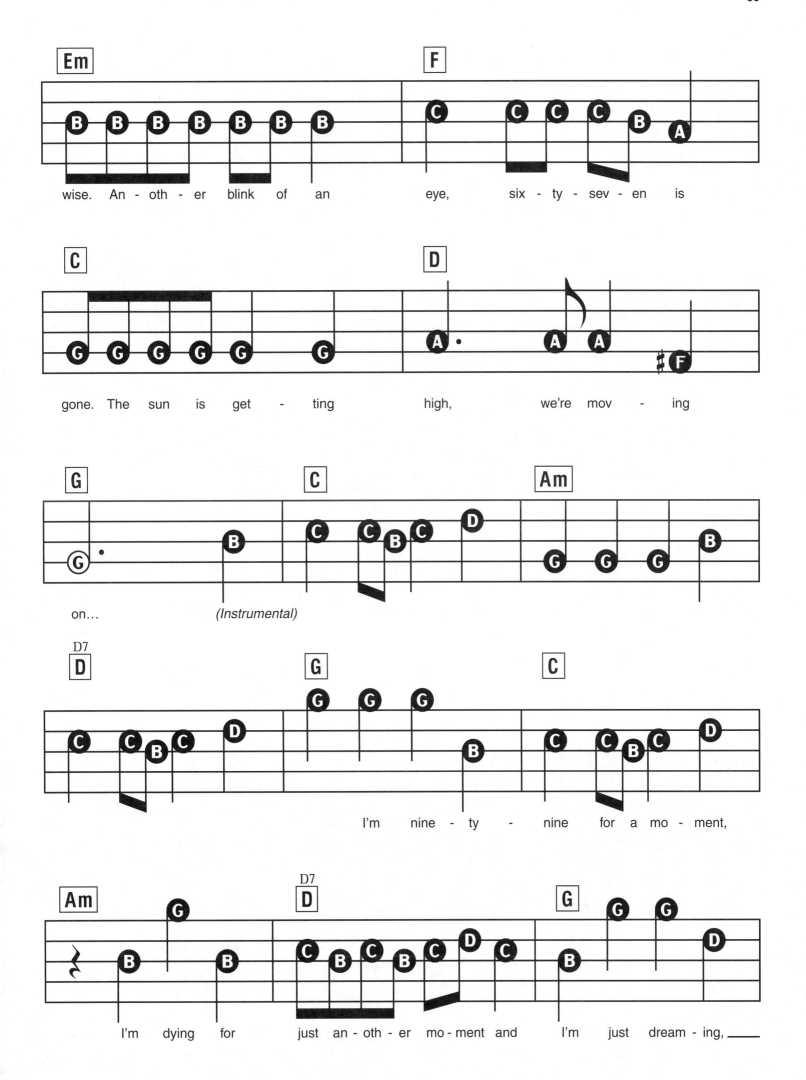

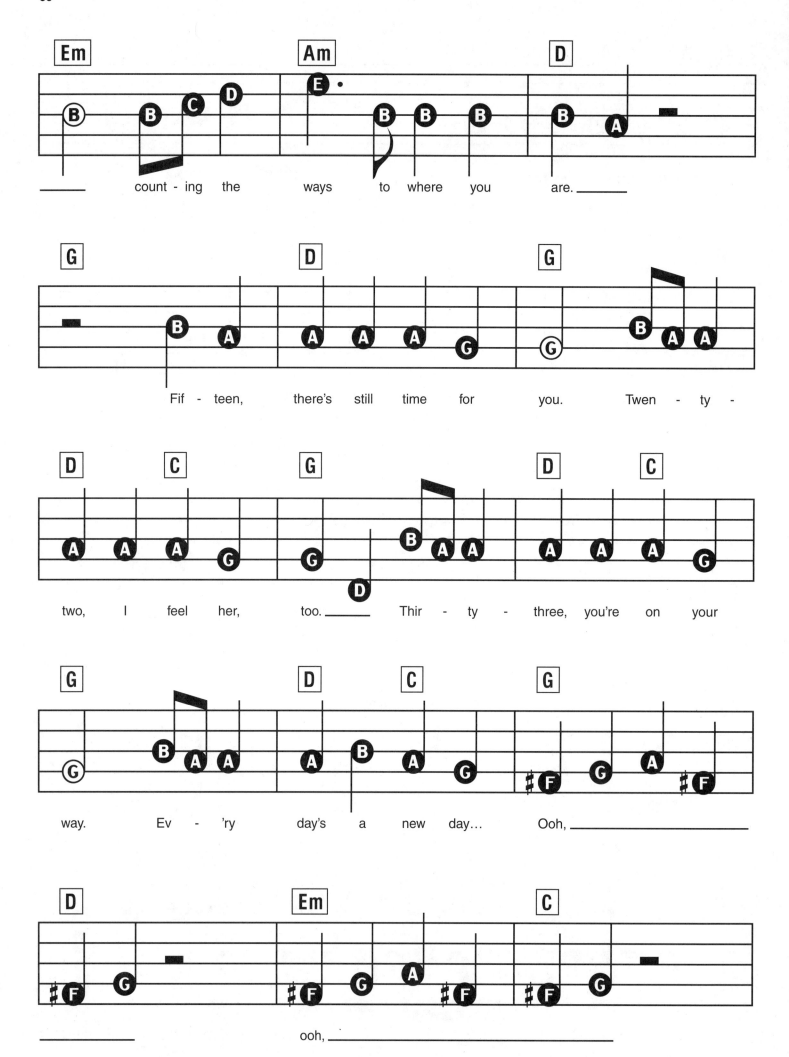

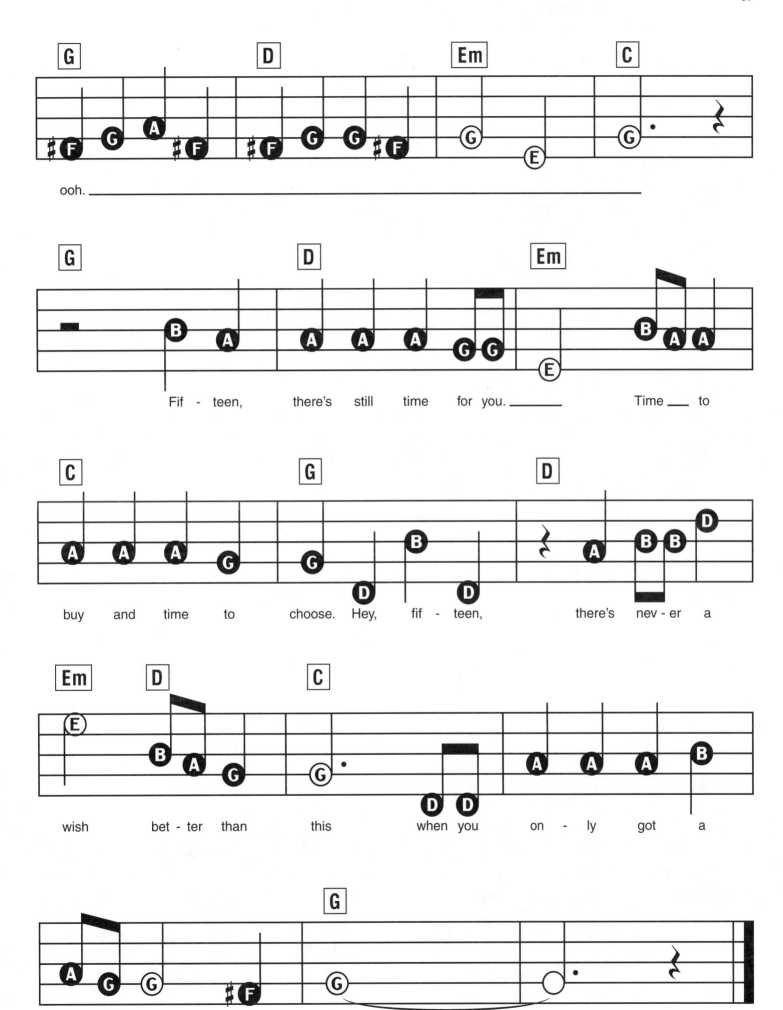

ooh. _____

Fif - teen, there's still time for you._____ Time __ to

buy and time to choose. Hey, fif - teen, there's nev - er a

wish bet - ter than this when you on - ly got a

hun - dred years to live. _____

Ribbon in the Sky

Registration 2
Rhythm: 8-Beat or Rock

Words and Music by
Stevie Wonder

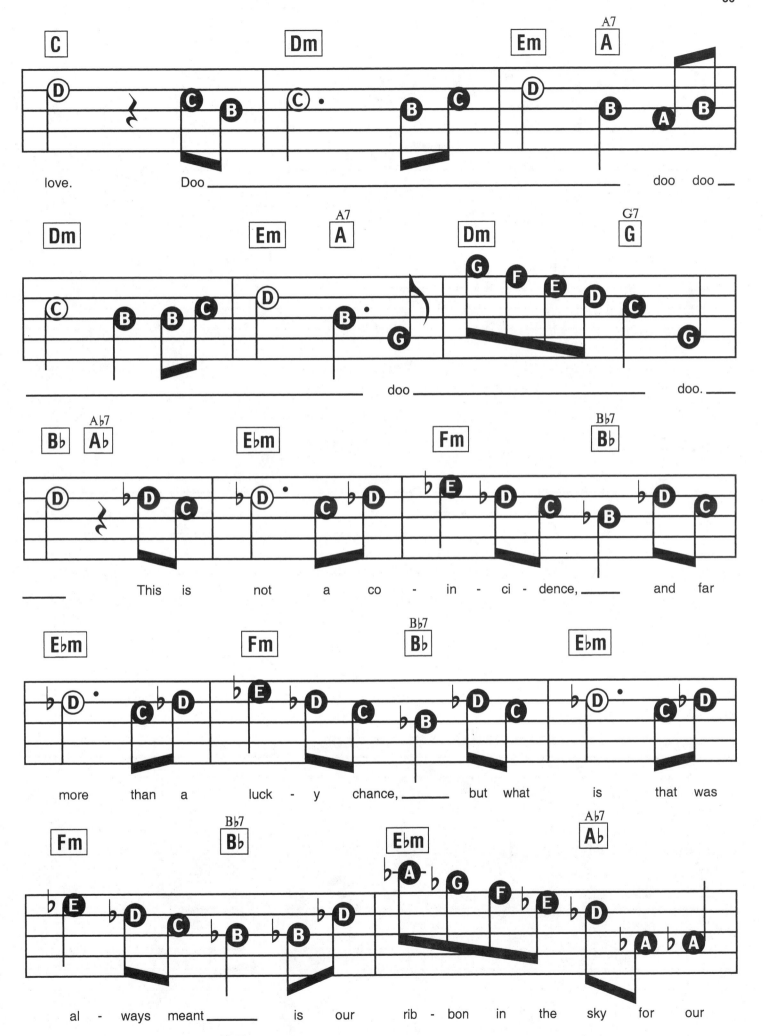

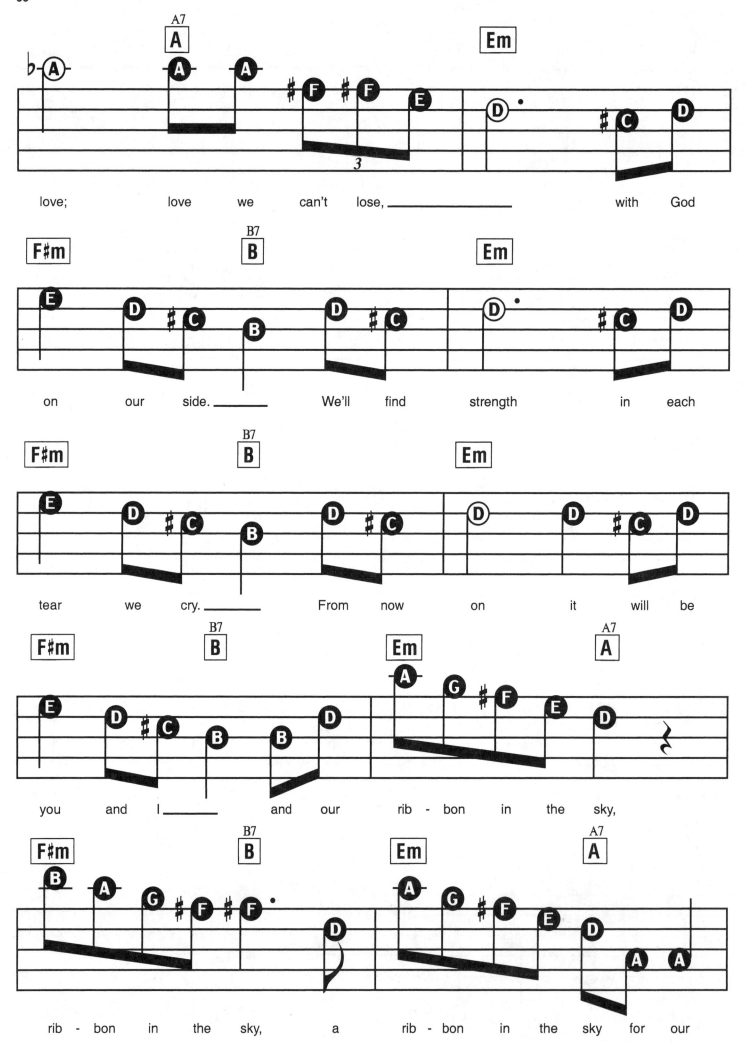

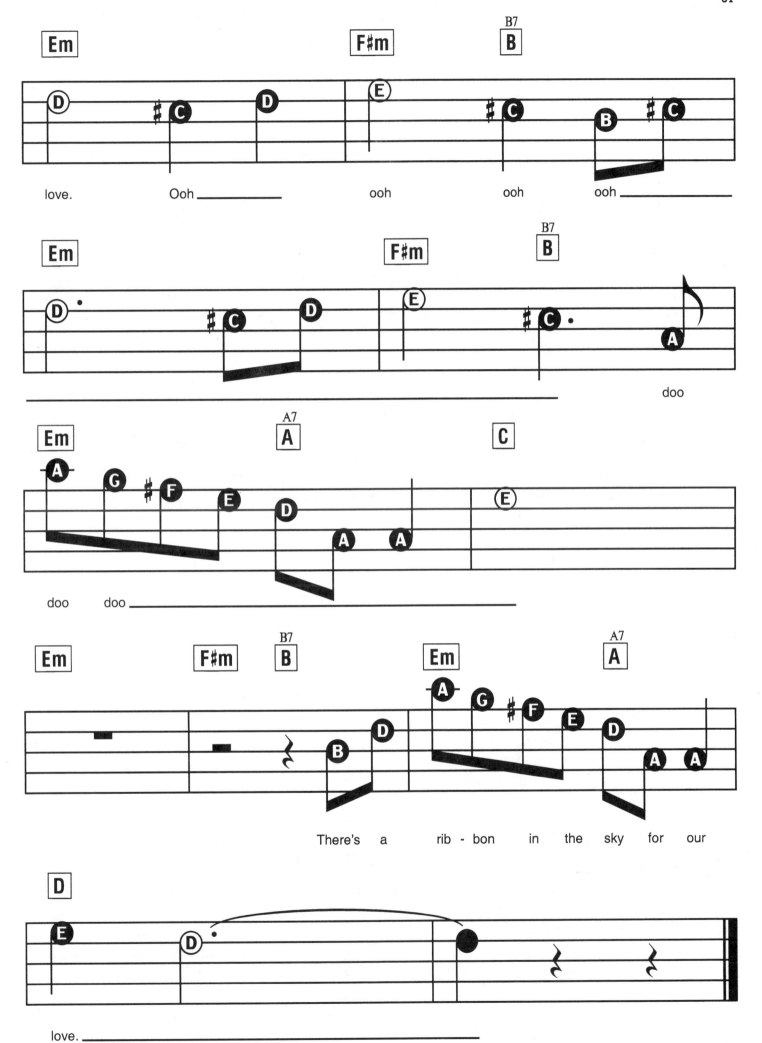

A Thousand Miles

Registration 4
Rhythm: Rock or Dance

Words and Music by
Vanessa Carlton

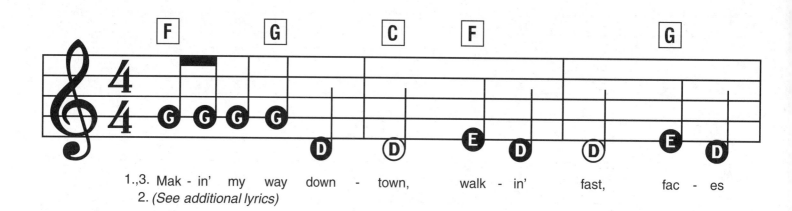

1.,3. Mak - in' my way down - town, walk - in' fast, fac - es
2. (See additional lyrics)

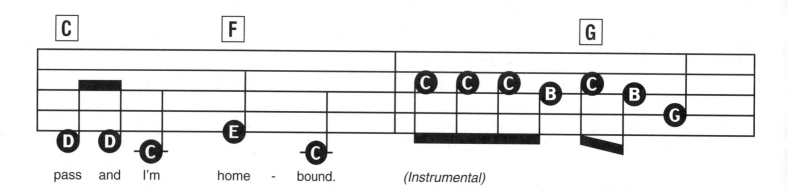

pass and I'm home - bound. (Instrumental)

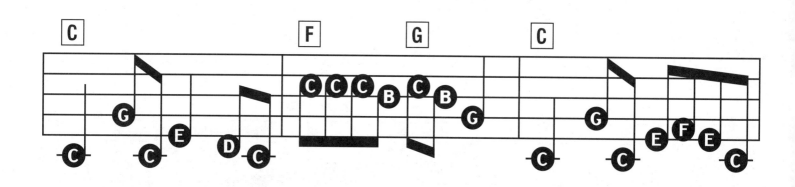

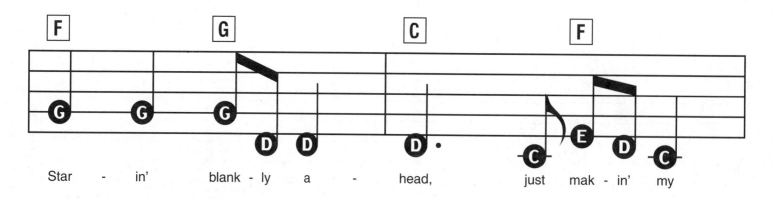

Star - in' blank - ly a - head, just mak - in' my

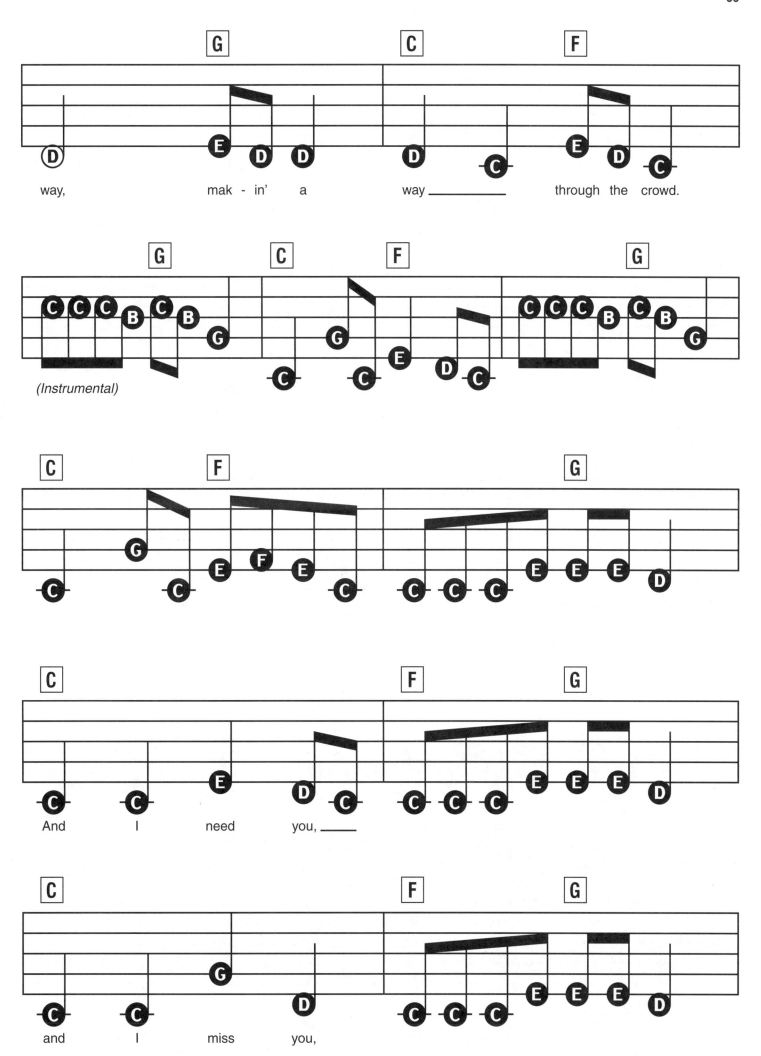

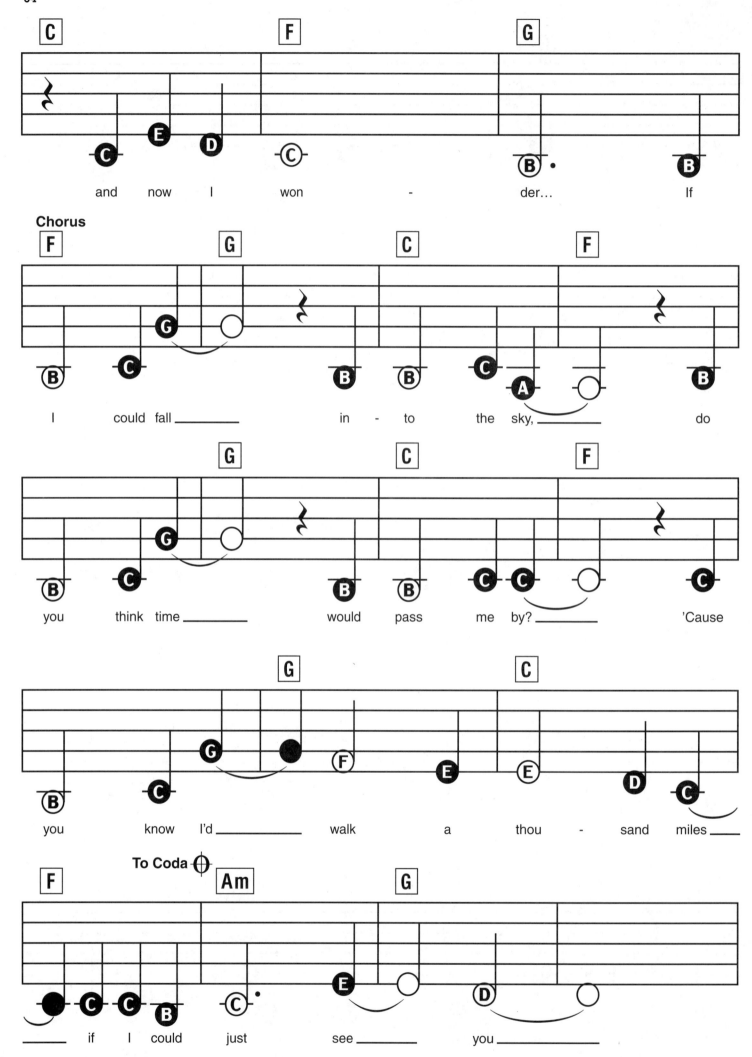

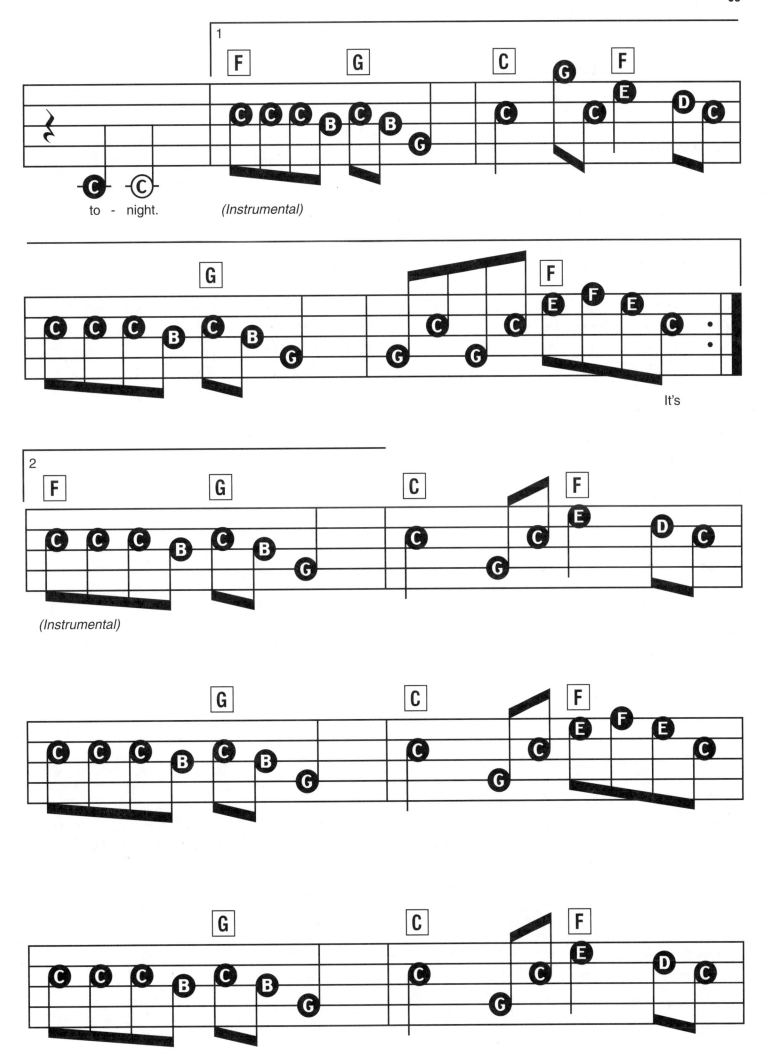

96

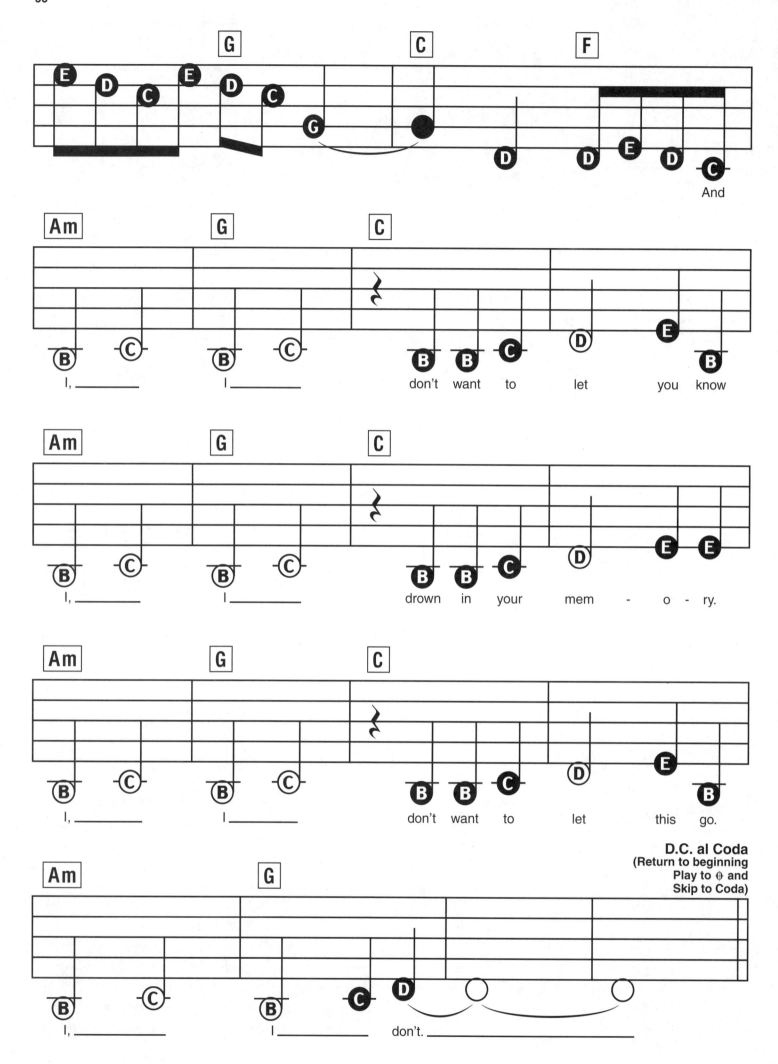

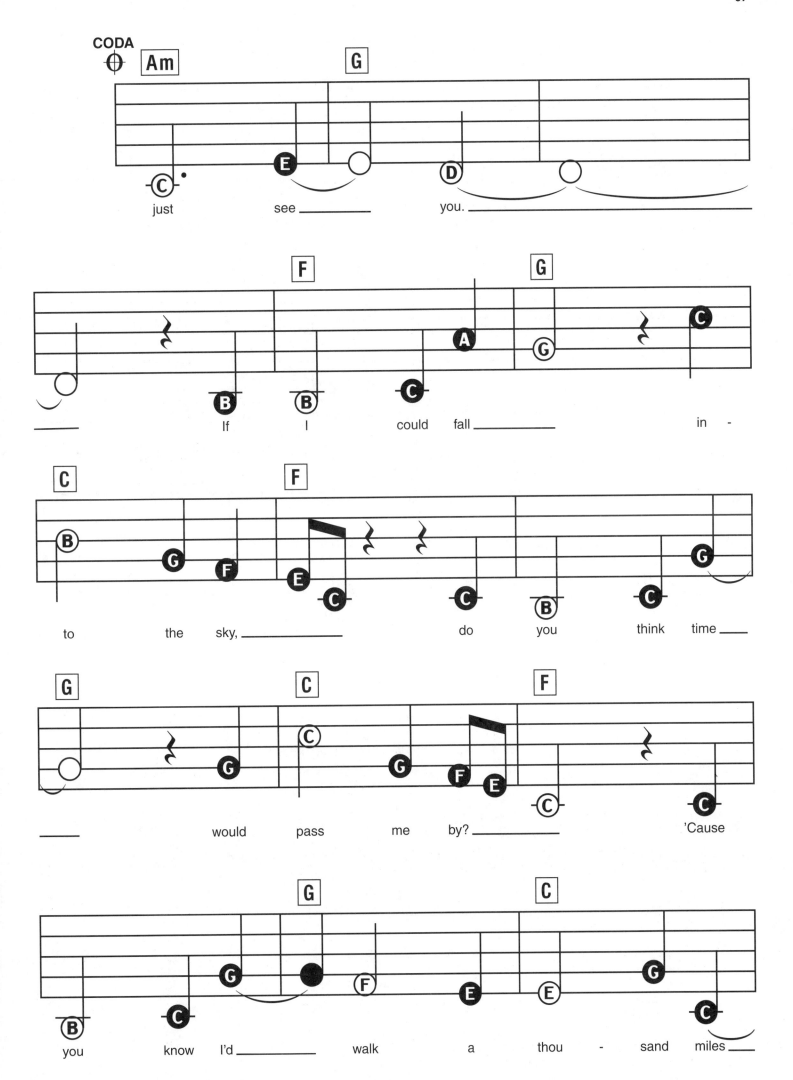

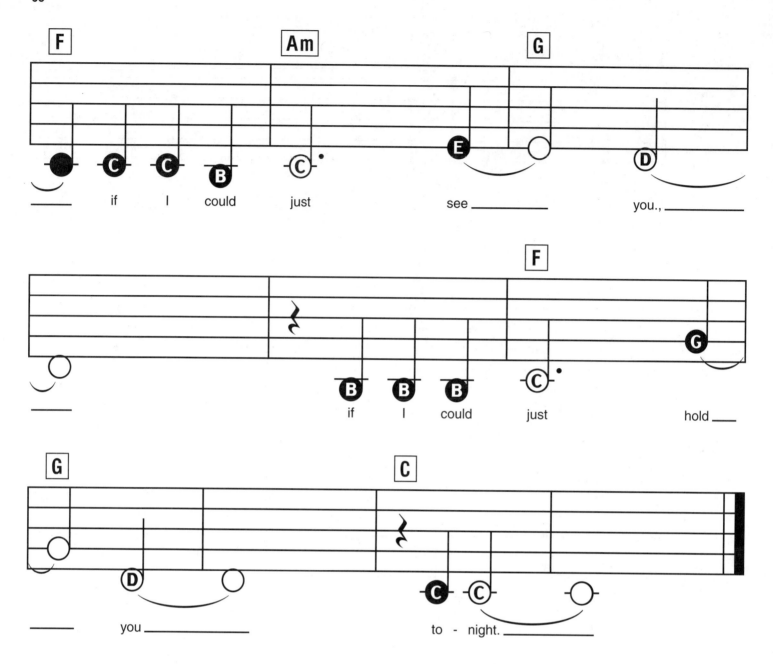

if I could just see _____ you., _____

_____ if I could just hold ___

_____ you _____ to - night. _____

Additional Lyrics

2. It's always times like these when I think of you
   And wonder if you ever think of me.
   'Cause everything's so wrong and I don't belong
   Livin' in your precious memory.
   'Cause I need you,
   And I miss you,
   And I wonder…
   Chorus

Wonderful Tonight

Registration 4
Rhythm: Pops or Rock

Words and Music by
Eric Clapton

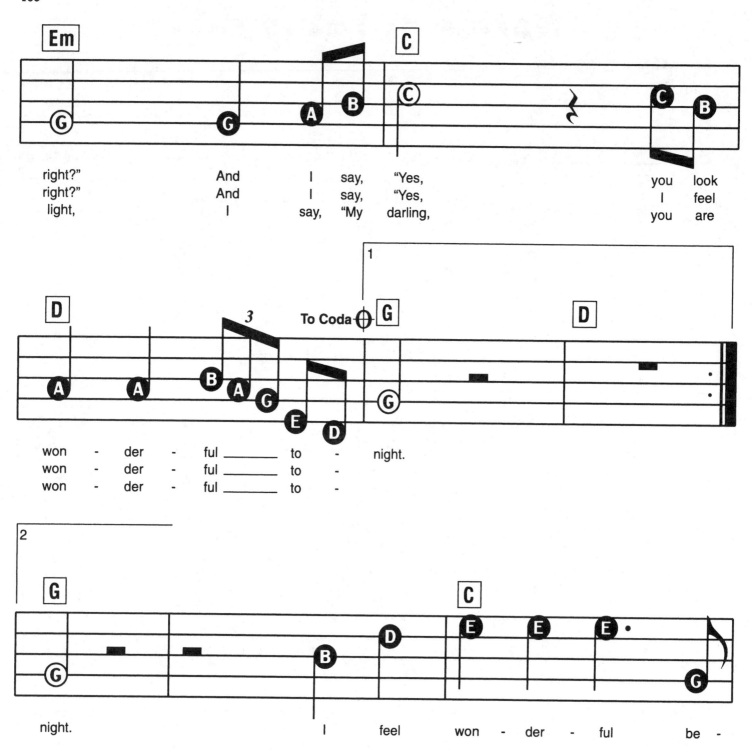

right?" And I say, "Yes, you look
right?" And I say, "Yes, I feel
light, I say, "My darling, you are

won - der - ful _____ to - night.
won - der - ful _____ to -
won - der - ful _____ to -

night. I feel won - der - ful be -

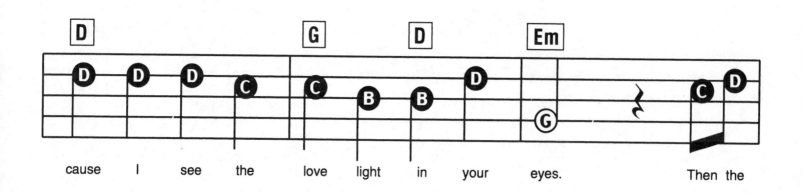

cause I see the love light in your eyes. Then the

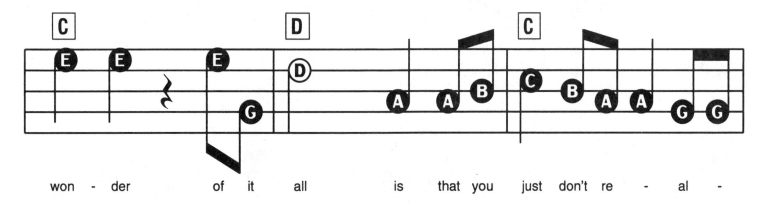

won - der   of it all   is that you just don't re - al -

D.C. al Coda
(Return to beginning
Play to ⊕ and
Skip to Coda)

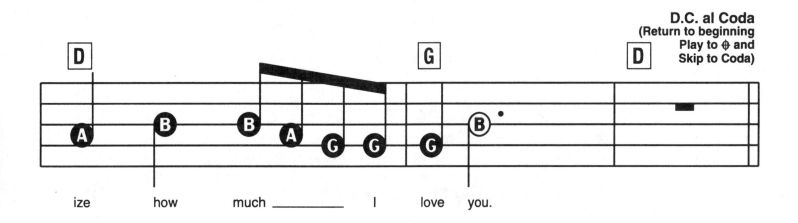

ize   how   much _____ I   love you.

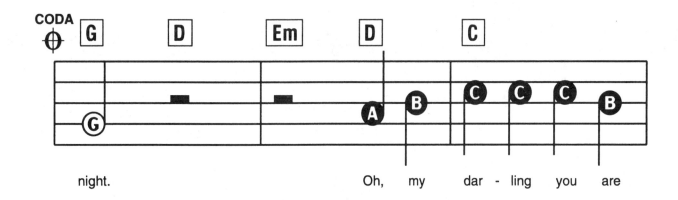

night.   Oh, my dar - ling you are

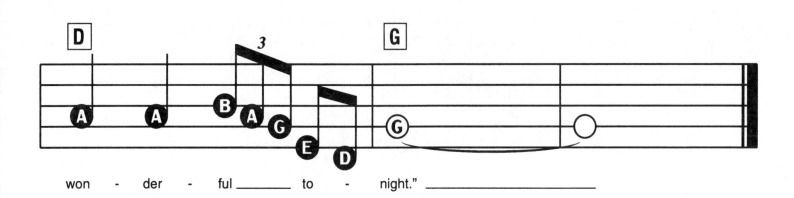

won - der - ful _____ to - night." _____

Walking in Memphis

Registration 4
Rhythm: Folk or 8-Beat

Words and Music by
Marc Cohn

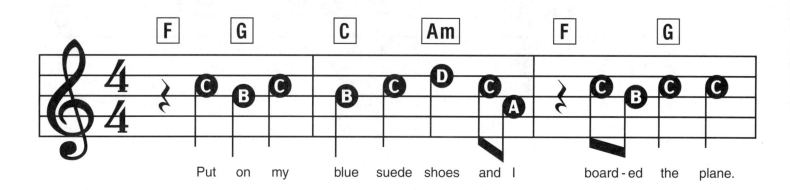

Put on my blue suede shoes and I board-ed the plane.

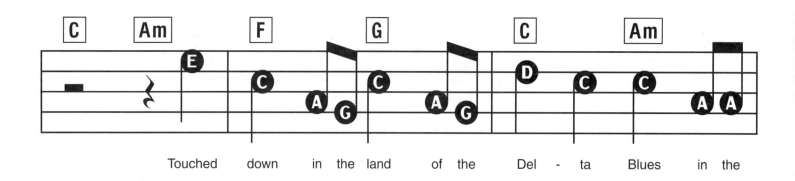

Touched down in the land of the Del - ta Blues in the

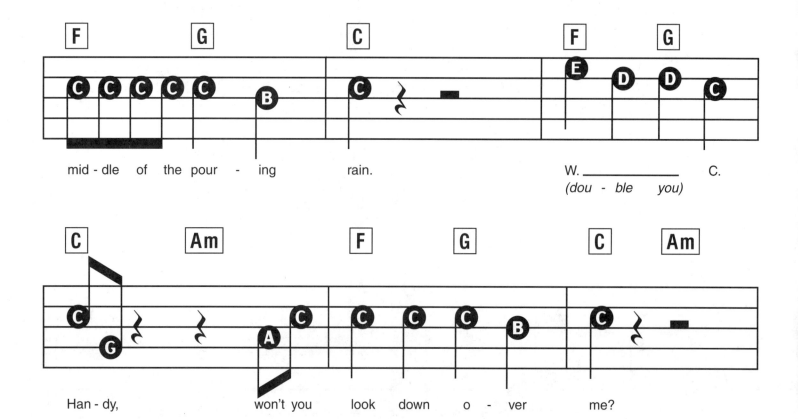

mid - dle of the pour - ing rain.   W. _____ C.
                                     (dou - ble you)

Han - dy,   won't you look down o - ver me?

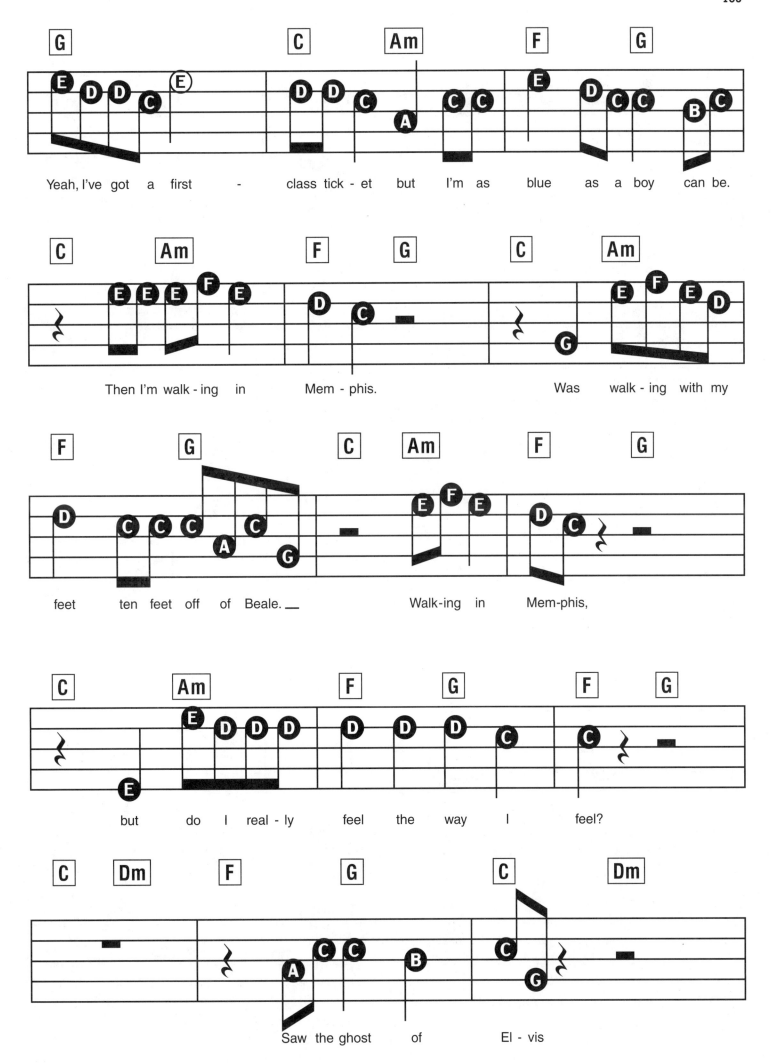

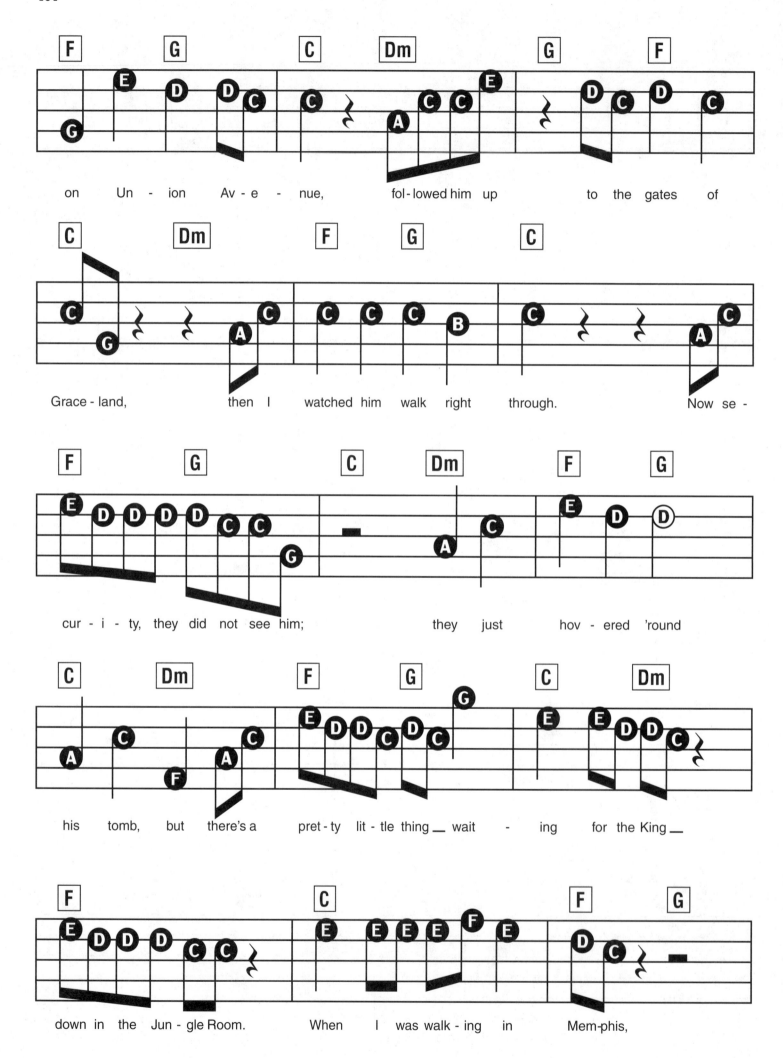

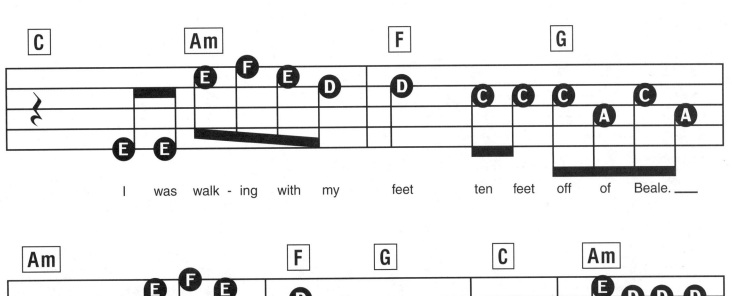

I was walk-ing with my feet ten feet off of Beale. ___

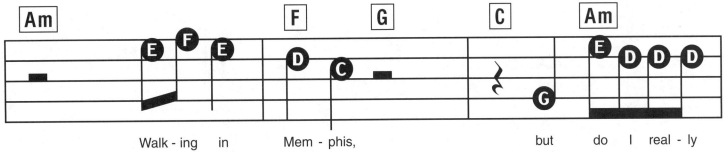

Walk-ing in Mem-phis, but do I real-ly

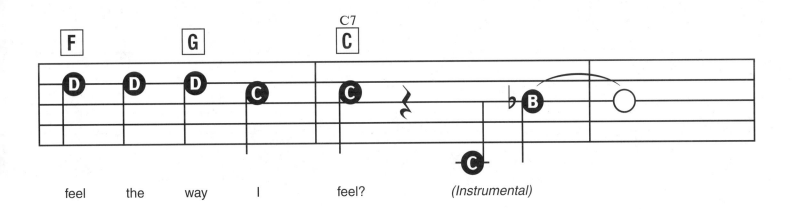

feel the way I feel? *(Instrumental)*

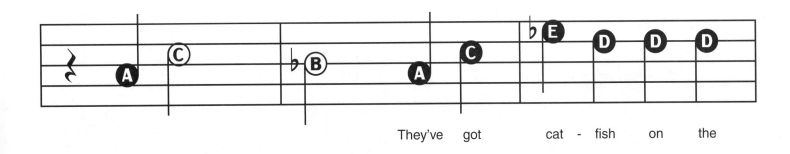

They've got cat-fish on the

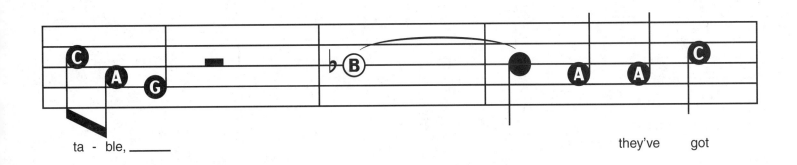

ta - ble, ___ they've got

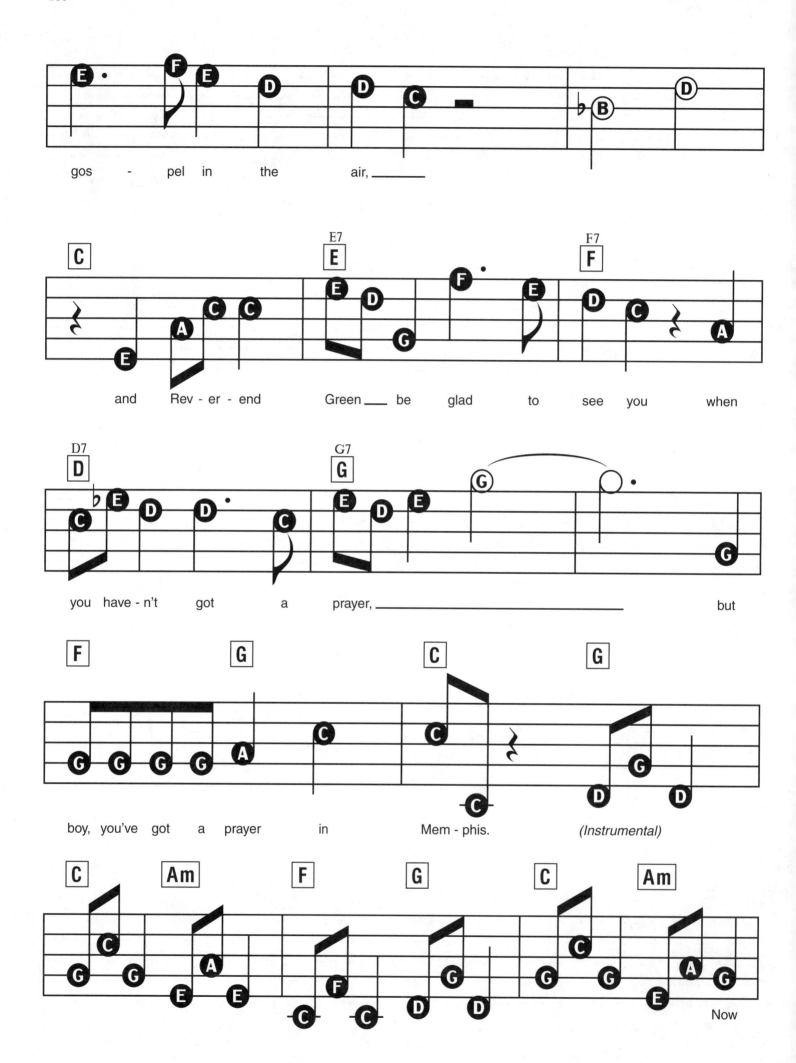

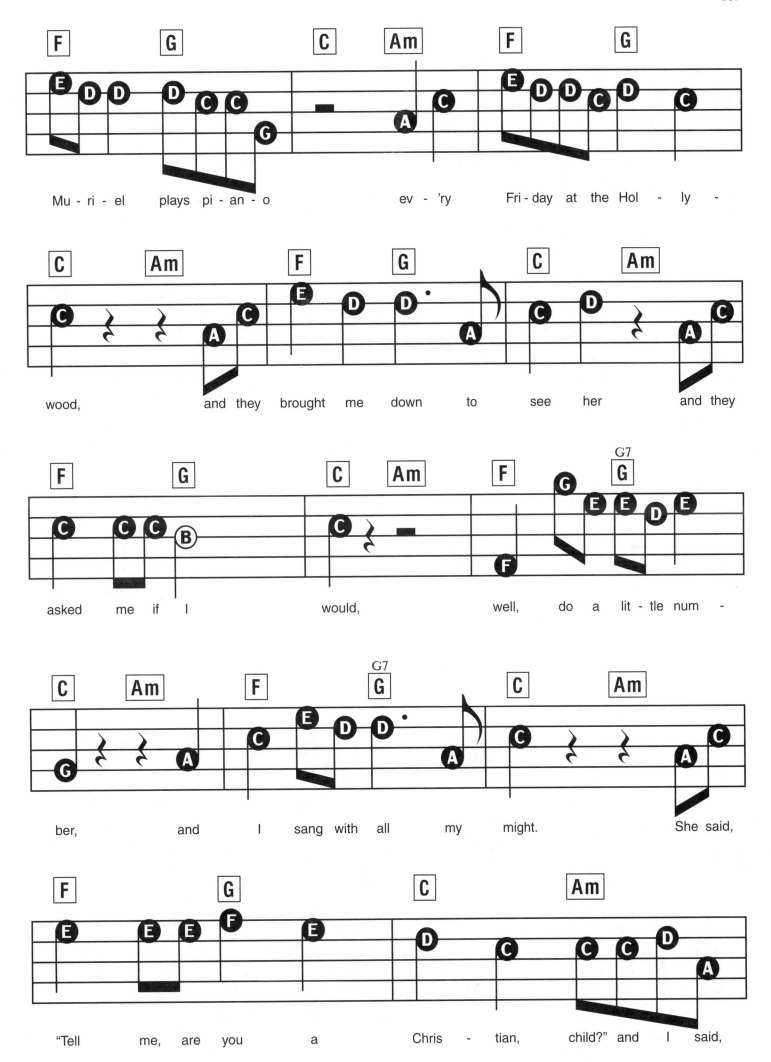

108

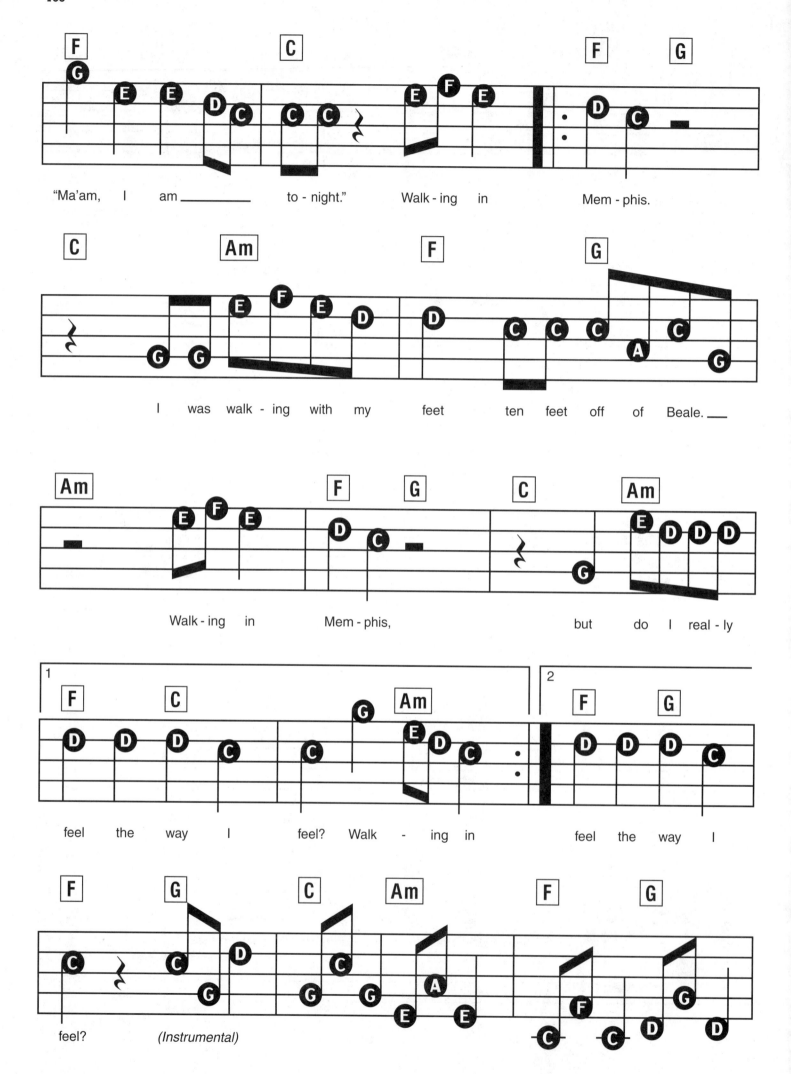

We've Only Just Begun

Registration 1
Rhythm: 8-Beat or Pops

Words and Music by Roger Nichols
and Paul Williams

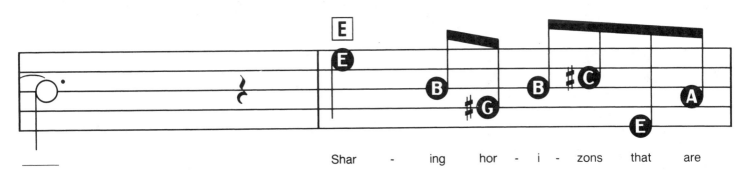

Shar - ing hor - i - zons that are

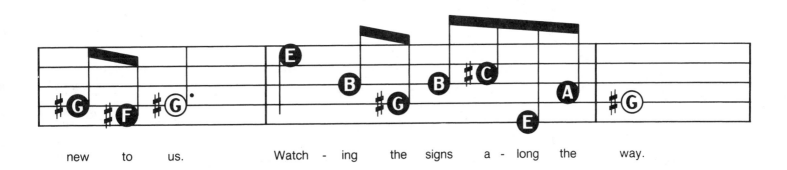

new to us. Watch - ing the signs a - long the way.

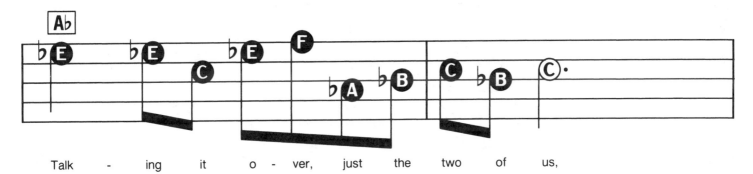

Talk - ing it o - ver, just the two of us,

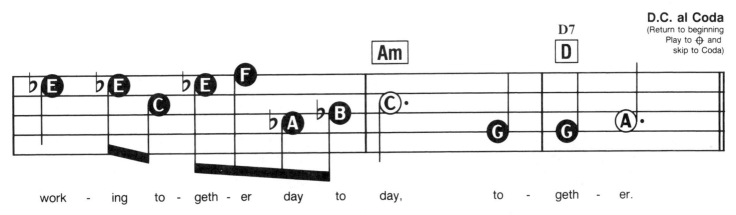

work - ing to - geth - er day to day, to - geth - er.

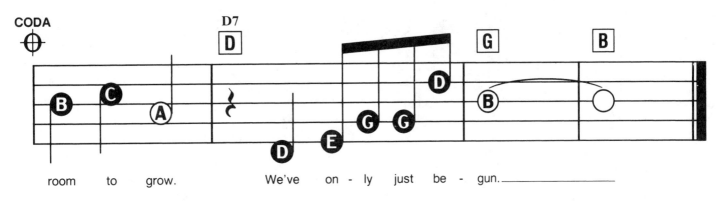

room to grow. We've on - ly just be - gun.

You Are So Beautiful

Registration 1
Rhythm: Pops or 8-Beat

Words and Music by Billy Preston
and Bruce Fisher

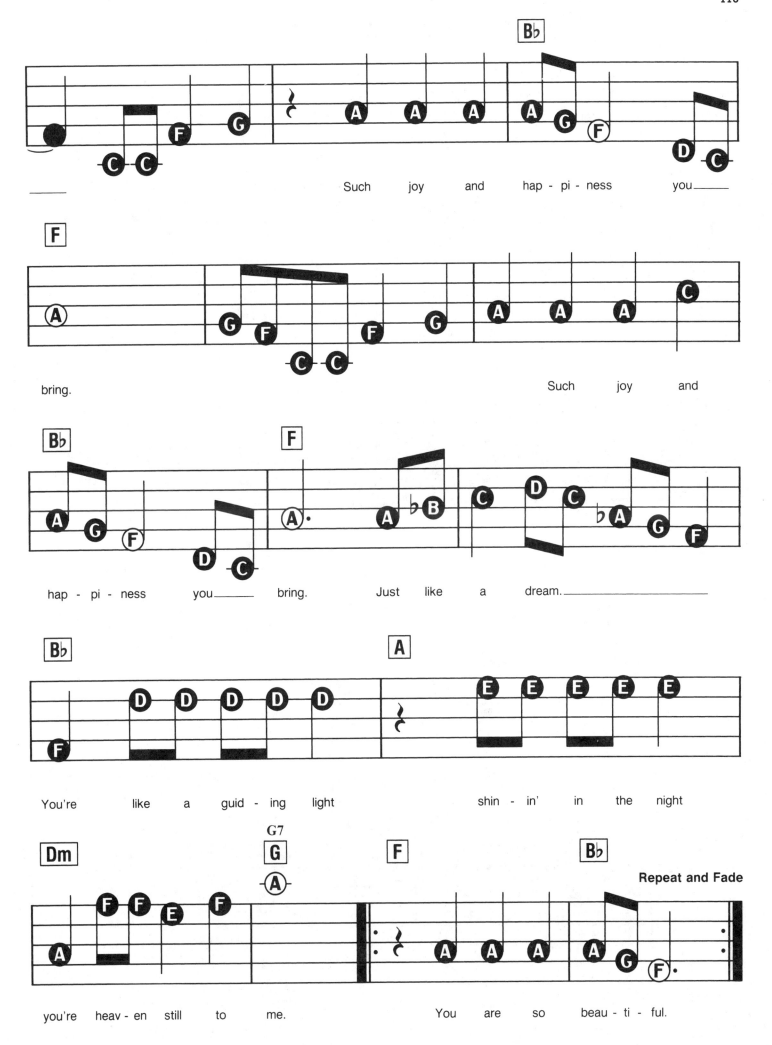

Your Song

Registration 3
Rhythm: Swing or Pops

Words and Music by Elton John
and Bernie Taupin

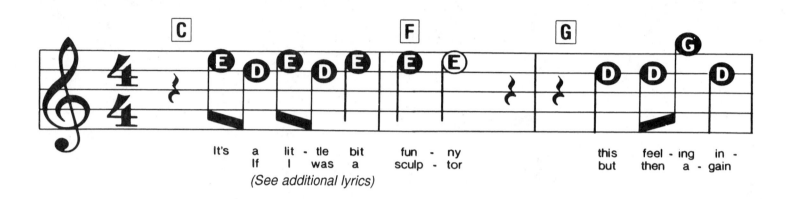

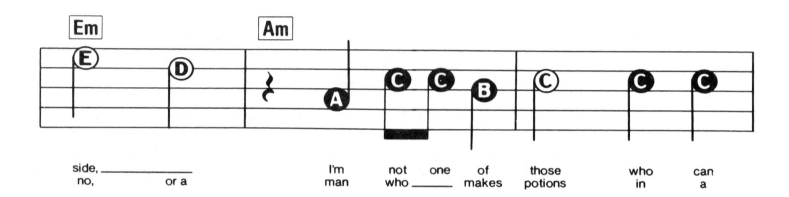

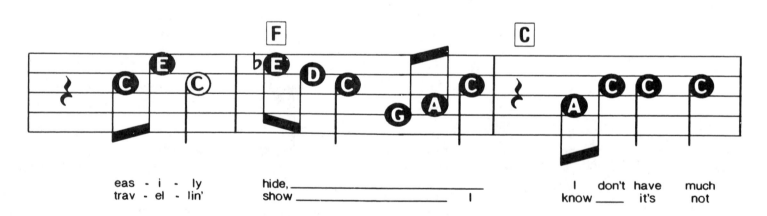

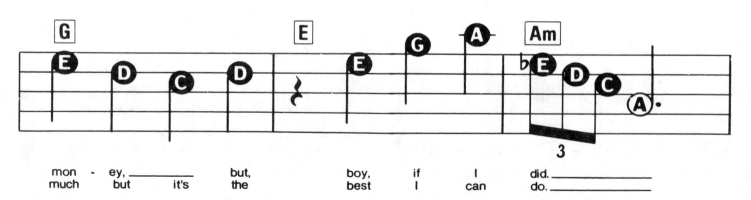

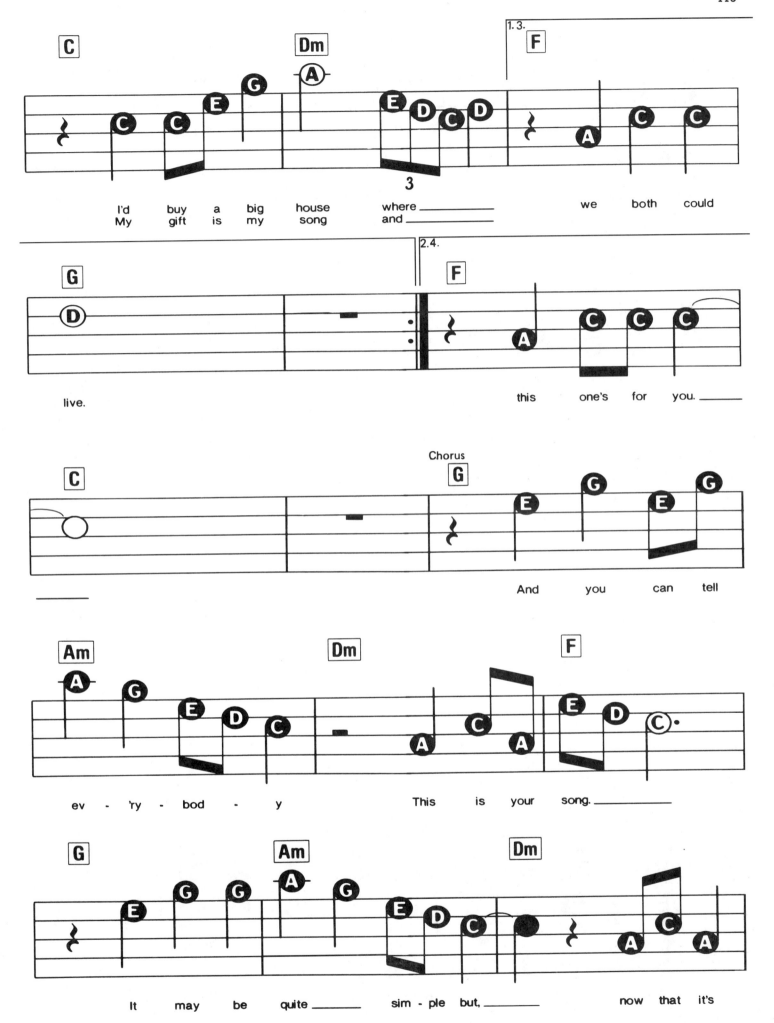

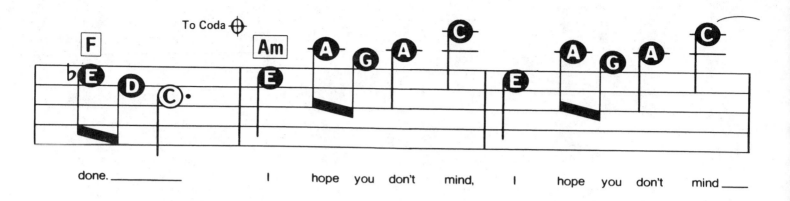

done._____ I hope you don't mind, I hope you don't mind _____

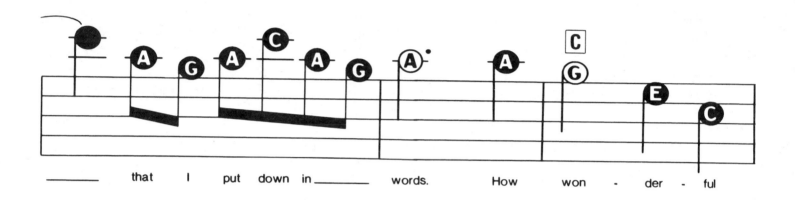

_____ that I put down in _____ words. How won - der - ful

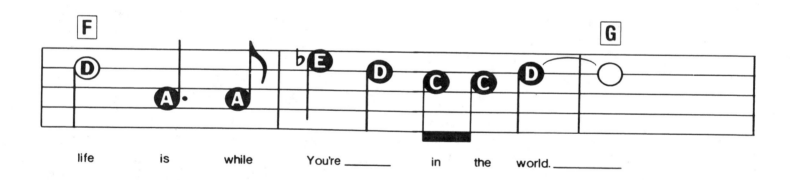

life is while You're _____ in the world. _____

D.C. al Coda
(Return to beginning, take 3rd & 4th endings, Play till ⊕ and skip to Coda)

⊕ CODA

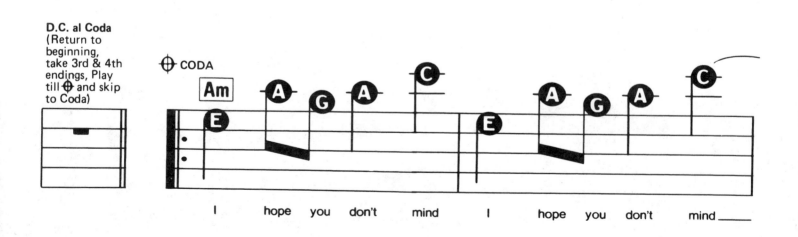

I hope you don't mind I hope you don't mind _____

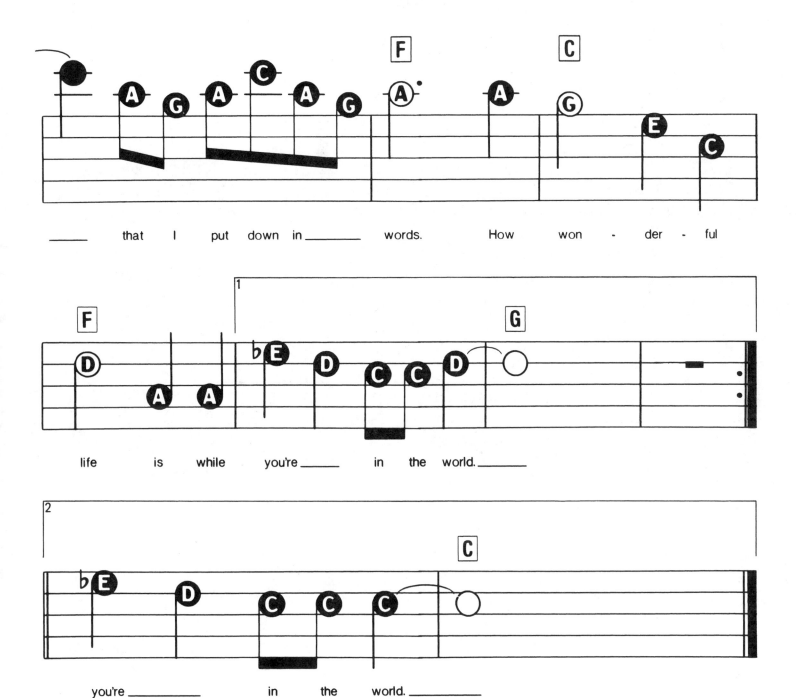

that   I   put down in _____ words.   How   won - der - ful

life   is   while   you're _____ in   the world. _____

you're _____   in   the   world. _____

Additional Lyrics

3. I sat on the roof and kicked off the moss.
   well a few of the verses, well they've got me quite cross,
   But the sun's been quite kind while I wrote this song,
   It's for people like you that keep it turned on.
   Chorus

4. So excuse me forgetting but these things I do
   You see I've forgotten if they're green or they're blue,
   Anyway the thing is what I really mean
   Yours are the sweetest eyes I've ever seen.
   Chorus

You Raise Me Up

Registration 3
Rhythm: Ballad

Words and Music by Brendan Graham
and Rolf Lovland

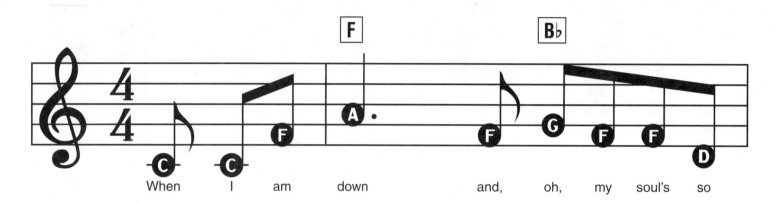

When I am down and, oh, my soul's so

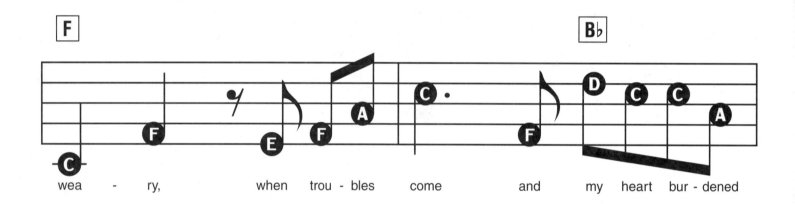

wea - ry, when trou - bles come and my heart bur - dened

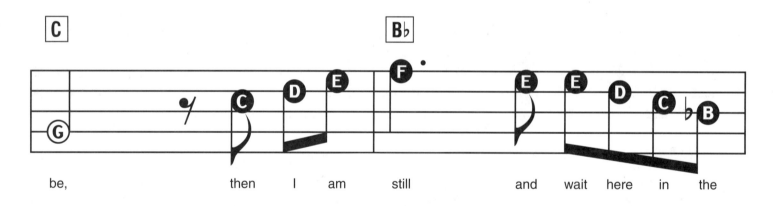

be, then I am still and wait here in the

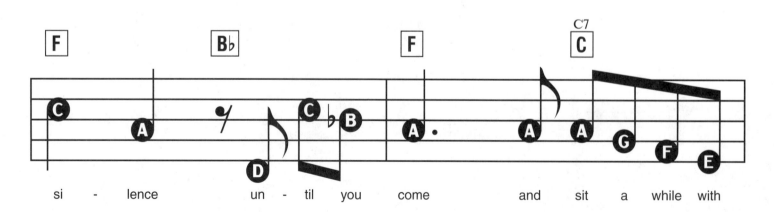

si - lence un - til you come and sit a while with

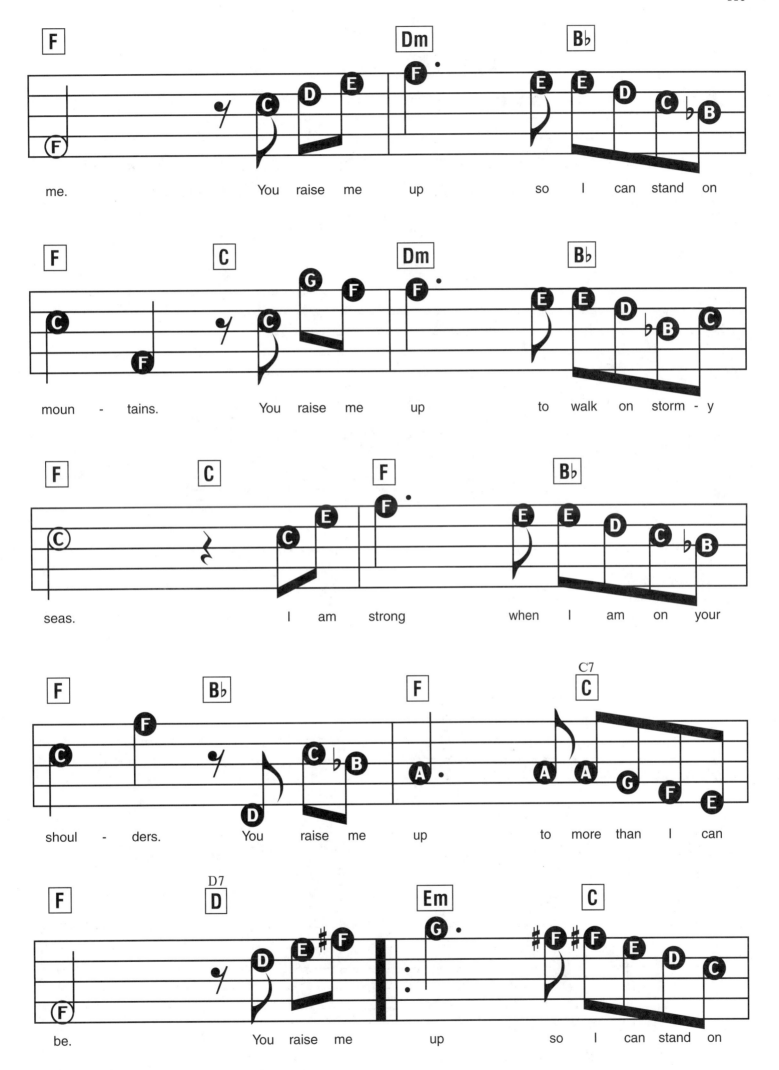

120

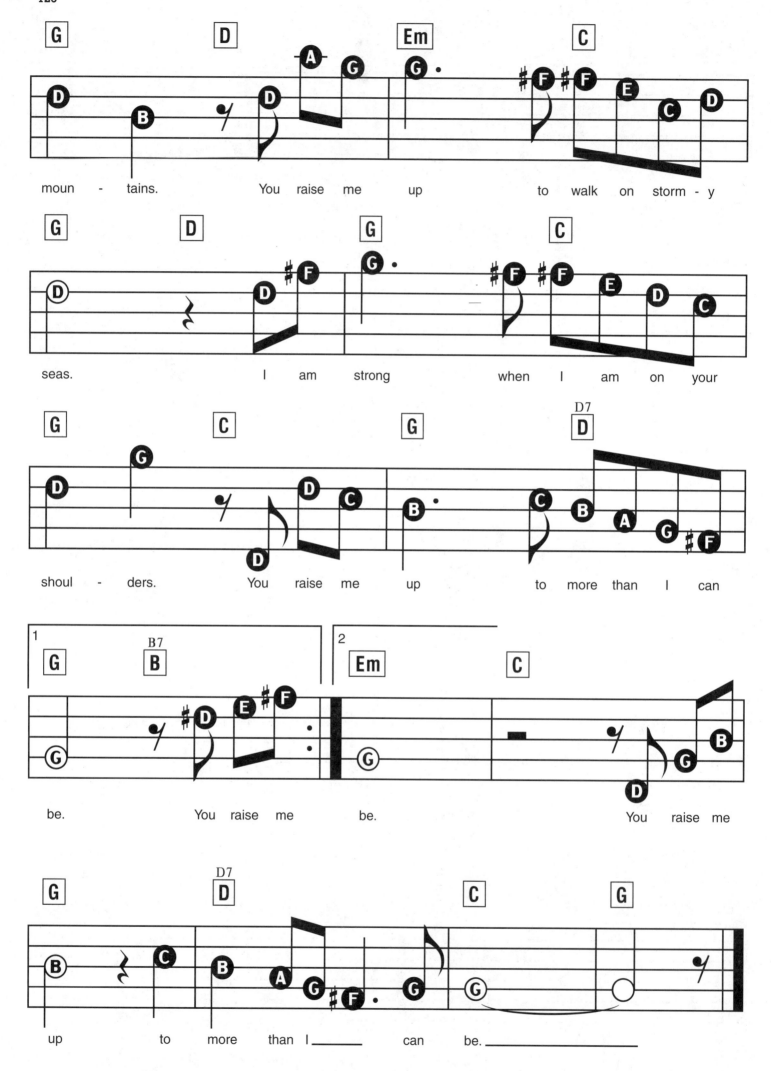